June Durant is a retired teacher, a member of the Jane Austen Society of the UK and an amateur genealogist. She enjoys traveling—once hitchhiking around the coast of the Iberian Peninsular and into North America, living and working for ten years in Africa and twice sailing around the world—on a container ship and some years later on a cruise ship.

June lives in Berkshire, close to her twin daughters, and thus delights in being part of her four grandchildren as they grow into adulthood.

For Sue, Pippa and Jenny
whose belief and encouragement are ever present.

June Durant

JANE AUSTEN IN THE THAMES VALLEY

AUSTIN MACAULEY PUBLISHERS™

LONDON • CAMBRIDGE • NEW YORK • SHARJAH

A CIP catalogue record for this title is available from the British Library.

ISBN 9781035849291 (Paperback)
ISBN 9781035855988 (ePub e-book)

www.austinmacauley.com

First Published 2024
Austin Macauley Publishers Ltd®
1 Canada Square
Canary Wharf
London
E14 5AA

Thank you to my sister Janet, daughters Pippa and Jenny, and friend Sue, who were my occasional and willing companions on the several trips that were the basis for the three excursions.

Table of Contents

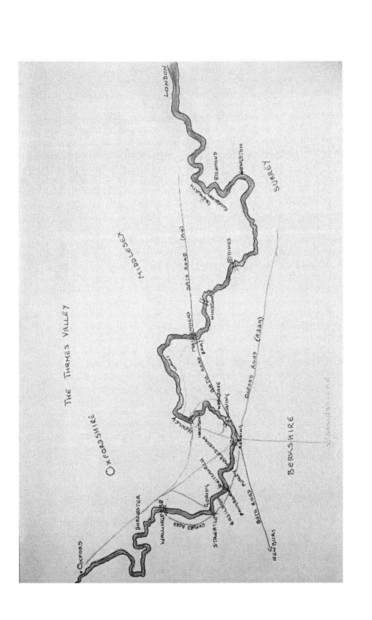

THE THAMES VALLEY

OXFORDSHIRE

OXFORD

DORCHESTER

WALLINGFORD

STREATLEY • GORING

PANGBOURNE

READING

HENLEY

MARLOW

COOKHAM

MAIDENHEAD

BRAY

WINDSOR

STAINES

MIDDLESEX

BATH ROAD (A4)

OXFORD ROAD (A329)

OXFORD ROAD

BATH ROAD

NEWBURY

BERKSHIRE

HAMPTON

TEDDINGTON

RICHMOND

KINGSTON

SURREY

LONDON

By the same author:

The School in a Wood
Searching for Words in Jane Austen
Another Search for Words in Jane Austen

For Sue, Pippa, and Jenny,
whose belief and encouragement are ever-present.

'What is it *worth of human life, unless it is woven into the life of our ancestors, by the records of history?'*

– Marcus Tullius Cisero

The Background

Halfway through the eighteenth century, three young ladies had been close friends for several years. Mary, Cassandra, and Caroline met at each other's houses, at social gatherings, and at other public events where young ladies might expect to meet with a future husband. Mostly they met in Henley, but often in Reading. Occasionally, the Leighs at least, would go on an excursion to Oxford where they had relations living and/or studying. All of them went to London and to Bath for the season.

This friendship extended to Cassandra's sister Jane and her brother James. Cassandra, James, and Jane were the children of Thomas Leigh, vicar of St Margaret of Antioch in the village of Harpsden, just two miles out of Henley towards Reading, on the Oxfordshire bank of the River Thames.

Caroline Girle had recently moved to Caversham, which was situated on the Oxfordshire bank opposite Reading. Mary lived at Henley Park with her Newell parents. Henley Park was owned by Gislington Cooper, who also lived in Henley, at Phyllis Court. The Coopers were very much part of this social scene and the son Edward and daughter Ann were friends of Cassandra, Mary and Caroline. Although living a little outside Henley, on the Maidenhead road on the

Berkshire side of the river in the ancient village of Hurley, the East family were amongst the group of families who met up in each other's houses and at social occasions in Henley and Reading.

Another family who were firm friends of these young people were the Powys boys whose home was at Hardwick House in Whitchurch, which was on the Oxfordshire bank of the river opposite Pangbourne. The Leighs may have known the Powys family before they came to Harpsden, for both families had roots in the Midlands where a century earlier they had been supporters of the beleaguered Stuarts. Whether this was the case or not, the children of the two families became very close friends and grew up together. Within this group were the Freemans from Fawley Court on the Marlow Road in Buckinghamshire, and the D'Oyleys at Greenlands. Occasionally, they met up with the Stonors of Stonor Park, a more private family who remained loyal to the Roman Catholic religion. All these homes were within easy riding distance of each other.

Whilst the girls were busy preparing for the big step into marriage, simply enjoying each other's company at social gatherings, or walking in this pleasantest of spots in the Thames Valley, the boys were in various stages of their studies at Oxford University. These eligible young men were James Leigh, Philip and Tom Powys, Edward Cooper, Ralph Cawley, William East, perhaps George Birch and others of the local well-to-do families such as the Freemans at Fawley Court. Those at St John's gathered other friends into the group who came from other parts of the country. One of these was George Austen who had won a scholarship at Tonbridge Grammar School.

Can't you just imagine these young sprigs entertaining their family in Oxford or going home for the vacation, perhaps taking their friend George with them as he had no real home to go to, socialising in each other's homes or at the Freemans at Fawley Court, the D'Oyley's of Greenlands, the Stonors too, each of them with a past that connected them to the Royalist cause but, apart from the Stonors and old Theophilus Leigh in Oxford, now embraced the Church of England. I can see a lawn sweeping down to the Thames (still in existence), peopled in the eighteenth century by young ladies and gentlemen and their elders, strolling by the river or relaxing in the shade after a late breakfast that had followed a celebratory ball that didn't end until the early hours of the morning. Perhaps they talked of well-known figures of the day who had connections in the town, Mr Walpole's next visit. Perhaps it was of the return to college, plans of a visit to Bath, the coming London season or simply talk of a future together. Whether it was here in this idyllic spot by the Thames, or in Oxford, London or in Bath, romance blossomed.

Caroline Girle found her husband amongst the local well-to-do families. She married Philip Lybbe Powys and took up residence at Hardwick House where she had often visited. When Mary Newell married George Birch, they moved out of the area, eventually to Windsor. Ann Cooper perhaps found her husband in Henley. She married Ralph Cawley. Cassandra's brother James probably found his bride elsewhere (London, perhaps?). She was Jane Cholmeley who had been born in the West Indies sent back to England to be educated and to find a rich husband. She certainly did that. Jane, Cassandra's beautiful sister, married Edward Cooper, who had taken holy orders. As to Cassandra, our heroine of this part of the story, everyone expected her to marry her childhood friend Tom Powys but she fell in love with Tom's college friend, the clever and handsome George Austen.

And so, the first half of the seventeenth century passed; the 1760s saw a new king on the throne and our heroines and their heroes, married and perhaps started a family, scattered along the Thames Valley or further afield, but they never lost touch with each other. Some were to continue the friendship and family ties in a more tangible form. They all wrote letters, some of which survived, even published; some wrote journals, one of which was preserved and published in an abridged form; occasionally, they visited each other at their new marital homes. In some instances, the offspring were visitors too. Indeed, there was to be intermarriage between the children. We, hungry for every scrap of evidence, devour any mention of their doings from whatever source it may come, because of their connection to Jane Austen, the catalyst and central heroine of this story. Most of all, we want to know if Jane Austen met them, wrote to them, or visited them. In the Thames Valley particularly, the snippets of genuine evidence are all too tantalising and few. Most live only in our hopeful imaginations.

What Happened to Them?

<u>William East</u>: Sir William East, a college friend of George Austen, sent his son Gilbert to Mr Austen in Steventon, to be prepared for entrance to the university. When Sir William died in 1815, his son became Sir Gilbert who had no issue. In later life, Gilbert visited James Edward Austen Leigh at his home in Scarlets and probably entertained the Austen Leighs at Hall Place. It is unlikely that Jane ever visited them in Hurley, although her father George Austen may quite well have done so.

<u>Mary Birch, nee Newell</u>: Mr and Mrs George Birch eventually went to live at Barton Lodge at St Leonards Hill, in Windsor. Mary Birch was a prolific, lively and entertaining letter writer many of which were exchanged between her and her lifelong friend Cassandra Austen nee Leigh. We know that Jane Austen visited her at least once, and hoped to on occasions (Letters 64, 105, 106) – but not in Henley. We also know that she liked her mother's friend very much (Letter 91). Mary lived until she was a hundred years old, and her letters written in the last two years of her life were electronically published (and possibly in the public domain) some years later and referred to the offspring of her earlier friends.

Ann Cawley nee Cooper: When Ann Cooper married Ralph Cawley of Henley-on-Thames, they went to live in Oxford where Ralph eventually became Master of Brasenose. After he died, Ann became a tutor to her niece Jane Cooper and Jane's cousins Cassandra and Jane Austen. There is no evidence that Ann Cawley taught other girls besides these three and it is a mystery why she was entrusted with them in the first place. Maybe she was looking for additional income after her husband died. Although they had not been short of cash, Ann did not benefit from her husband's will. Perhaps it was because she was resident in the seat of learning and the fact that Theophilus Leigh was still alive and James Austen was studying and therefore resident there, may also have had a bearing on the decision. The girls had been with Mrs Cawley for only a few months when she suddenly whisked them off to Southampton, for no apparent reason unless because it was a spa town, it was cheaper there, she had friends or relations living there or as some writers say, to escape an outbreak of measles – with tragic results. For details see the many biographies of Jane Austen. When Ann Cawley died in 1787, she was buried in Henley. Her brother Edward Cooper was executor of her Will but he never carried out those duties – perhaps because he saw her as the author of his wife's death and it was left to his son Edward to do so.

Caroline nee Girle and Philip Lybbe Powys: Caroline is best known for her diary. Emily Climenson, compiler of an abridged version, misleadingly names her as Mrs Lybbe Powys. In fact, Lybbe was Philip's second name, not his double-barrelled surname. The name of Lybbe was given to him in recognition of his mother's maiden name (a practice still carried out today). This misinterpretation on the part of Mrs Climenson reflects the careless editing of the diaries with some unreliable results and omissions concerning Jane Austen. When Caroline married Philip, she moved from her home in Caversham to take up residence at Hardwick House, a country estate belonging for many generations to the Lybbe family. It came under the ownership of the Powys when Philip's father married the daughter Caroline Lybbe. Philip and the younger Caroline (Girle) had a clutch of children, one of whom we will meet later. As the children grew, Hardwick House was handed over to the eldest son and the now elderly Powys retreated to Fawley where brother Tom held the Living. Did Jane Austen meet Mrs Powys when she was a schoolgirl in Reading (1784/5 to 6/7)? We will never know. It doesn't appear to be recorded in the diary and one would have thought a treat like that would have been. However, Caroline did record that she entertained the two Miss Austen's for dinner at Fawley during the time the Austen ladies visited the Coopers at Harpsden in 1799. In 1792, Caroline and Philip went on an excursion to the Isle of Wight with Dr Edward Cooper and his daughter Jane, stopping off at Basingstoke on the way. However, her diaries do not record any meeting there between them and the Austens who lived a stone's throw away at Steventon although they did meet up on the way home when the Austens shared breakfast with them at the Wheatsheaf Inn at Popham.

Philip Lybbe Powys died in 1809 and Caroline moved to East Street in Henley. She died in 1817 at Fawley having gone there to comfort her daughter-in-law after her son Thomas Powys had died. Caroline was buried with her husband at Whitchurch.

Tom Powys: Tom grew up in Hardwick House and was part of the group who socialised in the two local towns of Reading and Henley as well as the fashionable haunts of London and Bath. He was also up at Oxford. The Leighs were particular friends as well as other lads up at Oxford at the same time as James. In the seat of learning, the group of fellow students included George Austen, a one-time pupil and then briefly Usher (equivalent to Deputy Head) at Tonbridge Grammar School, before continuing his studies at Oxford in 1761. Although expected to marry Cassandra Leigh, Tom gave way to his clever and handsome friend and officiated at the marriage of the pair in Bath – to whence the Leighs had removed – following the death of Cassandra's father.

By this time, 1764, Tom had been given the Living, amongst others, of Fawley. He became Dean of Canterbury where he went mostly to live in the Cathedral Close, although retaining the Living in Fawley, sometimes returning to the Rectory, now lived in by his brother Philip and wife Caroline. Whilst staying with her brother at Godmersham, Jane was a fellow diner with the Dean in Canterbury hosted by Mrs Knight. When Tom died, he was buried at Whitchurch. He never married.

Jane nee Leigh and Edward Cooper: The beautiful and socially accomplished Jane, married Edward in 1768. Edward was given several Livings and at the time of the birth of their son Edward, Edward and Jane Cooper were living in Southcote, a small village on the Bath Road just west, nowadays part of Reading. Jane's sister Cassandra, now Mrs Austen, visited them there with her two sons James and Edward. The Coopers then went to live in Bath. It was their daughter Jane who was to be educated with her cousins, Cassandra and Jane Austen first with Ann Cawley (Edward's sister) in Oxford. When Ann Cawley took the girls to Southampton, they contracted typhus (probably), which Mrs Jane Cooper caught when she and Sister Cassandra rescued the girls from this spa town, and from which she died. Distraught, Edward Cooper then retreated to Sonning in his beloved Thames Valley where he lived until his death. His daughter Jane continued her education with her cousins, now at the Abbey School in Reading. After her mother's death, Jane Cooper spent more time with the Austens in Steventon than she did with her father in Sonning. Indeed, she was married at Steventon Church with George Austen officiating. She may have met her husband, Thomas Williams, if or when she went to the Isle of Wight with the Austens (although there is no evidence that the Austens ever visited the island) or most likely when she accompanied her father and the Powys on their visit in 1792. After she became Mrs (later Lady) Williams, Jane died tragically in a carriage accident. Albeit Sonning is a neighbour of Reading, there is no evidence that Jane Cooper ever took her cousins Cassandra and Jane Austen to her home there.

Edward Cooper junior, Jane's brother, was also ordained and became curate at Harpsden where his mother had been born and grew up. (The Living was in the gift of the Powys family). He had married Caroline Powys, daughter of Philip and Caroline. From curacy, he moved to take up the Living in Hamstall Ridware in Staffordshire (in the gift of the Leighs).

Dr Edward Cooper senior was vicar of St Andrews, Sonning until his death in 1792, soon after his trip to the Isle of Wight with the Powys.

James Leigh later Leigh Perrot: James married Jane Cholmeley. They spent their married life between their home 'Scarlets' in Hare Hatch (in the Parish of Wargrave, which borders the River Thames not far from Sonning) and Bath. Their increasing wealth, their lives and their relationship with the Austens is well documented in various biographies and articles. James Leigh Perrot died in 1817. His wife lived on until 1836 aged 92. Both were buried in the same plot at Wargrave. The estate was inherited by their nephew, James Austen's son, who became James Edward Austen Leigh (J.E.A.L.), Jane Austen's first biographer.

Cassandra Austen nee Leigh: Cassandra was one of the few amongst her friends who did not find her husband in the local community. (Her brother James and friend Mary Newell, for example, were others) It is generally recognised that Cassandra met George Austen on one or more of her many visits to Oxford where she had relations, her uncle Theophilus Leigh being the most noteworthy. Upon her marriage, Cassandra was whisked away to Hampshire where she is widely believed to have lived a quiet life bringing up her lively and intelligent family. However, she did travel, including to her home in and around the Thames Valley, especially when her firstborn boys were young and later when George Austen owned his own carriage. For almost thirty years, the Thames Valley had been home to Cassandra Leigh. She returned there on visits, not just with her young boys but later in life with her daughters Cassandra and Jane, specifically to Harpsden.

Jane was there – or was she?

There are three categories that can be applied to this question: a) definitely, b) speculation on possibility and c) never. To consider the answers, I will follow the map of the Thames, tracing its course from Whitchurch in Oxfordshire in the west to Hurley in Berkshire in the East.

Whitchurch (Hardwick House): As we have seen, this was the home of the Powys family and it was familiar to Jane's mother Cassandra. However, we can place this in the 'never visited by Jane' category. It is possible that she passed it if she travelled to Oxford via Reading on what is now the A329 – still known as the Oxford Road. I think Mrs Austen, proud of her own Leigh inheritance, would have recounted the support given to the Royalist cause by the Lybbes. Across the river from Whitchurch is Purley Hall, situated on the Oxford road in Berkshire, where Warren Hastings awaited his trial in 1788. This residence had close connections with its near neighbour Basildon Park, recently featured as Netherfield and which had a brief appearance in the BBC2's marking the 200th anniversary of Jane's death. The owner of Basildon Park, Sir Francis Sykes, brought Warren Hastings' son back to England and handed him over to Mr and Mrs George Austen.

Reading: This falls easily into the 'definitely visited by Jane' category for here she was at school. The Jane Austen Society has placed a plaque near the spot where the school once stood. Jane and her brother Henry, stayed in Reading overnight in 1813 when in Letter 85 she warns: "I should not wonder if we got no farther than Reading on Thursday evening." It is 'possible' that Reading was a stop-over for her on other occasions and she mentions it in *Sense and Sensibility*. Eleanor and Marianne are travelling with Mrs Palmer and Mrs Jennings. They 'wondered whether Mr Palmer and Colonel Brandon would get farther than Reading that night' indicating that Jane was familiar with the town as a staging post.

Did Jane Austen visit any of her relations whilst at school in Reading? Who knows? She was certainly taken out to tea by her cousin Edward Cooper and brother Edward Austen (later Knight) and a cousin of her mother's called in on his way home from London. Did anyone else take them out to tea? Caroline Powys, for instance, or the Leigh Perrots from Scarlets? Dr Cooper from Sonning? Some biographers have said that she definitely visited Sonning. But any visits that the Austen girls may have made whilst they were at school in Reading have not been recorded. Anything of this nature is pure speculation occasionally based on informed guesswork.

Sonning: Jon Spence was quite certain that Jane Austen visited her uncle-in-law when she was at school with his daughter and the vicar at Sonning. But Dr Cooper was a broken man after the death of his wife and possibly suffering from ill-health so not really up to entertaining young people. He seems to have been taken under the wings of Philip and Caroline Powys. As already stated, there is no evidence to confirm that Jane Austen visited Sonning and it is only speculation that she would have visited the home of her cousin with whom she was educated. Sonning is not mentioned in any of her letters.

Shiplake: Is opposite Wargrave on the Oxfordshire bank and has a marginal connection with Jane. It is where Emily Climenson, editor of *The Diaries of Mrs Lybbe Powys* lived in the vicarage. It is also where Lord Tennyson was married: he who wished to see the Cobb rather than other historical sites in Lyme Regis. I think we can safely assume that Jane never visited this village.

Hare Hatch (Wargrave): Mr and Mrs Austen and some of their children visited the Leigh Perrots at Scarlets. But there is no evidence to say that Jane did. This falls firmly into the 'speculative possibility' category. It is well-known that Jane loved Uncle James but not Aunt Jane. Was this dislike rooted in a childhood fear of a strict, straight-laced, childless woman? Did the Leigh Perrots convey the girls between Reading and Steventon – between school and home? The Leigh Perrots were certainly visitors to Steventon.

Harpsden-Henley: Here we are on safe ground again of the 'definite'. Letters confirm visits to Harpsden and Henley: Letter 18 when Jane refers to Edward Cooper's removal to Hamstall Ridware and Letter 85 when she tells Cassandra that 'We are to go to Windsor in our way to Henley'. Those extracts speak for themselves and there is no need for further elucidation except to refer you to Deidre La Faye's *Jane Austen's Letters*. Caroline Powys retired to live in New Street in Henley. Ann Cawley is buried in Henley and the Sarah

Hackett who is buried there is none other than Jane's other tutor, Mrs La Tournelle, aka Esther Bell.

Fawley: When Mrs Austen took her girls to her birthplace in order to visit the Coopers before they moved to Staffordshire, one would expect her to meet up with her lifelong friend, Caroline Girle now Mrs Powys. At the time, Philip and Caroline Powys were living in the remote village of Fawley, a few miles outside Henley on the Oxfordshire/Buckinghamshire border. Caroline Powys visited her daughter and son-in-law (Caroline and Edward Cooper) many times when they were living in Harpsden and one would expect her to make the effort when she knew that her friend Cassandra would be there, and diary entries confirm this. When I recently drove to Fawley from Henley, I left the main Marlow road and followed a delightful, winding route, mostly shaded by trees. It was uphill all the way and the narrow road leads to a quiet and secluded village. That route in 1799 must have been little more than a farm track so no wonder Mrs Austen did not travel there on that occasion. However, in her diary, Caroline tells us: "1799 September 2, Monday The Coopers to dinner and with them ye two Miss Austins & Mr W Warren." Fawley is a 'definitely visited' then. What a pity Cassandra was with her sister Jane as otherwise we may have had an excellent account of the event. Perhaps they were taken into the church to see the chancel that in 1748 John Freeman of Fawley Court had rebuilt with fittings from 'Cannons' the home of James Brydges, the first Duke of Chandos. As descendants of this illustrious person – through their mother – they would certainly have been interested. Unfortunately, the church was locked when I visited and I think closed for use, so if the fittings in the chancel are still the ones installed by John Freeman, I was unable to see them.

Hurley: We refer here to Hall Place which although in the Parish of Hurley, stands high above, a little distance away but overlooking the village. Sir William East owned Hall Place. He was at university with George Austen and sent his son, Gilbert to Steventon to be tutored by him, as did many of George Austen's college friends. George's time at Tonbridge under the caring attention of James Cawthorn had a positive effect. Had Cawthorn not suffered an untimely death in 1761 then it is likely that George Austen would eventually have become Headmaster at Tonbridge Grammar School. How different would Jane's life have been? I have no doubt that Cassandra Leigh would have married George Austen wherever he spent the rest of his life. Did Jane Austen visit Hall Place? Never, I think, but I do wonder if Mr Austen did.

Pilgrimage

We all want to visit the places where Jane Austen placed her footsteps or where she had the least connection. I could not have written this piece if I had not done so myself. I take with me my camera and a purse containing cash. However, I would here make a plea; give a caution; issue a warning. Many of these places are under private ownership. Scarlets, for instance, is now converted into private flats and the village of Fawley is quite reclusive. It is not a good idea to go knocking on doors or poking around private property. It is not possible to visit Hardwick House but a good view of it can be seen by walking the Thames Path between Pangbourne and Mapledurham. Phyllis Court is a Private Club (although I rather cheekily parked in their car park and walked down to the river) and Hall Place is now an agricultural college. Sometimes it is a good idea to just park the car and take a photograph. Visiting churches is another matter. The surroundings are always open to visitors. However, sadly, most of the churches themselves have to be kept locked these days. If you are fortunate and find one open, there is often a guide book which can be bought, brief histories or even post cards. Telephone numbers are displayed on boards outside so that visitors may make contact and possibly have the doors unlocked for them. As a courtesy, especially if you take photographs, it is only fitting that a contribution should be put into a collection box. Caution is all about speculation. Did she or didn't she? Beware of conclusions without evidence.

Three Excursions

Although these excursions begin in Henley or Reading, they can start in any of the places on the route. You may like to miss some and visit them at another time, making the excursion shorter, or even mix and match. Each spot can be visited singly without going to the others. There are stops which are only periphery to Jane Austen and can be left out altogether, for instance, Hurley and Hall Place may be missed or Phyllis Court; certainly Shiplake.

Here are the two proposed excursions which begin in Henley-on-Thames:

(I suggest you arm yourself with a local Ordnance Survey map or a large-scale road atlas.)

Henley (a)

Henry Austen was in *Henley* several times, the first recorded in 1796. In 1798, he was based there to train new recruits in his regiment. In 1813, he brought his sister Jane there, possibly in his capacity as Receiver-General for Taxes of Oxfordshire or maybe for a banking business. He visited his Cooper relations in Harpsden several times, riding there on his horse. At least once going on to Oxford, probably via Nettlebed and Wallingford.

Jane Austen would have passed through and possibly visited the town in 1799. She was there again in 1813 when no relations were living in the area. They possibly stopped at the Red Lion Inn – now very much changed – to rest horses or to partake of refreshment. Another alternative was The Catherine Wheel, both inns are still in existence.

Caroline Powys went to live at 35 New Street after her husband died and Jane may have visited her in 1813.

Using the centre as a hub:

Initially, proceed to *Harpsden* on the A4155 Reading Road. The road to the village is approximately 1½ to 2 miles on the right. Jane Austen's grandfather, Thomas Leigh, was vicar here from 1731 to 1764. His daughter Cassandra was born here and baptised in the church. She was to become Jane Austen's mother. Jane's cousin Edward Cooper became curate at this church until his move to Hamstall Ridware.

Jane, Cassandra and Mrs Austen visited Harpsden in 1799. Other members of the Austen family visited here from time to time.

Return to Henley and continue to Phyllis Court and Fawley on the A4155 Marlow Road. As you take the right fork on the mini-roundabout where the left goes to Wallingford and Oxford, you will pass Bell Lane on the right where Mrs La Tournelle ran her last school. *Phyllis Court* is a short distance outside Henley Town Centre on the right-hand side. It is possible to park, walk down to the river, and look upon the same scene as Cassandra, Jane and James Leigh did. Edward Cooper and his sister Ann Cawley lived here.

Their house was demolished so the one now standing is not the one that they knew.

Fawley is further along the A4155 and a road left leads to the village. <u>Tom Powys</u> was the rector here. <u>Caroline </u>and <u>Philip Powys</u> came to live here. <u>Jane</u> and <u>Cassandra Austen</u> dined here.

Assuming you set out in the morning, return to Henley where there are several good dining places for lunch.

Now for the second part of this excursion, which takes you to *Hurley*. Cross the Thames into Berkshire on the A4130 Maidenhead Road (which goes west to Oxford behind you). Hurley village is a turning left several miles along this road. There are commemoration plaques to <u>Gilbert</u> and <u>William East</u> in the church. Return to the main road, turn left and drive until a major roundabout leading to the M4 is reached. Take the second exit and a short distance further to Birchetts Green where Berkshire College of Agriculture is situated on the right. This is Hall Place and the home of <u>William</u> and <u>Gilbert East</u>, and the end of this excursion (a) so you may like to return to Henley for tea. I suggest at the River and Rowing Museum.

Henley (b)

From the Town centre, go over the bridge into Berkshire again. Immediately first right on the A321 to Wargrave; Hare Hatch and Sonning are further on, on the A4.

A road leading to *the Wargrave* church is on the right at the further end of the village. <u>James Leigh Perrot </u>is buried here. With the entrance to the church door on your right, just a few paces past it and on your left, you will find his impressive tomb where his wife is also interred. His wife Jane Leigh Perrott's plaque is to be found inside the church. There is also the grave of one of James Austen Leigh's sons – Arthur Henry Austen Leigh – who was a rector later in the nineteenth century.

Joseph Hill, lawyer to the Leigh family, lived in Wargrave. He accompanied the Austens to Stoneleigh Abbey.

Returning to the main street, turn right and continue until you reach the A4 roundabout. Turn left. A mile further along to Hare Hatch, *Scarlets Lane* (almost hidden) is signposted on the right-hand side. (If you reach The Bird in Hand on the left you have gone too far) Scarlets, the home of James and Jane Leigh Perrot and then of James Edward Austen-Leigh, is a little way up the road on the right, secluded by trees. A very private residence now.

Mr and Mrs Austen visited the Leigh Perrots here as did James, Edward, Charles, Francis and Henry Austen. When Mr Leigh Perrott died, Cassandra Austen visited to support her aunt. Cassandra visited at least once more just before her own death. James Edward and Caroline, the two youngest children of James, were sent to visit their aunt and later James Edward brought his wife Jane nee Smith (a Chute relation from the Vyne). There were probably more visits, of which we are unaware, by the Austen family but there is no record that Jane ever went to Scarlets.

Return to the A4 and turn left. Continue along the A4, over the roundabout and on to the next roundabout. Turn right to *Sonning*. Dr Edward Cooper, Mrs Austen's brother-in-law, was the rector here. His son, Edward Cooper junior, lived here when not at Eton or Oxford. His daughter Jane Cooper stayed here when not at school or with the Austens at Steventon.

Caroline Powys, daughter of Caroline and Philip, stayed here and married Edward Cooper junior.

You may like to pause for a snack or lunch at The Bull, situated close to the church and once a staging post which Jane Austen would have known even if she did not get out of the coach. Sit and contemplate!

Return to Henley by crossing the bridge at Sonning to the Oxfordshire side, continuing on the Sonning Road until it meets the A4155. At the roundabout, turn right to Henley. This road will pass *Shiplake* on the right. Mrs Emily Climenson, editor of *the Diaries of Mrs Lybbe Powys*, was the wife of the vicar here. Lord Tennyson was married here. Continuing along this road to Henley you will pass the left turning to Harpsden where the two expeditions from Henley began.

This third excursion begins in Reading.

Reading (c)

The Abbey ruins and site of Mrs La Tournelle's school is by Forbury Gardens and there is no guaranteed parking there. If you are driving from Henley, then follow the directions to the Queen's Road Car Park. From there, there is a long walk to the Abbey Gateway. Of course, if you have organised a coach trip you can all be dropped off at Forbury Gardens.

Reading Abbey. The Law Courts are next to the ruined abbey and are more or less built on the site of the Abbey School where Cassandra and Jane Austen and their cousin Jane Cooper went to school. By walking through the gateway from Forbury Gardens, a plaque can be found on the right, placed there by the Jane Austen Society. Discovering this long-lost site is like discovering Richard III under a car park.

Oscar Wilde was in the gaol next to the Abbey. Whilst there, he composed a recommended library list that included Jane Austen's novels. Mary Russell Mitford knew and described the Reading that Jane knew. She called it Belford Regis. Miss Russell is well-known for some remarks made by her about our heroine.

Do take time to explore the Abbey ruins. Whether the girls were allowed in those precincts is questionable but they could hardly be ignored.

Leave Reading by the A329 going west, which will take you to *Purley* and Pangbourne. There is a gentle down-hill that leads out of Purley and on the left-hand side is a stone gateway to Purley Hall. This is now a conference centre but was once the home of Warren Hastings whilst awaiting his trial for impeachment and before moving to Windsor where he lived during the trial. Continue along the A329 until you reach the first roundabout in Pangbourne. Turn right. There may be parking on the right where a Thames Path walk begins. If not, drive a little further under the bridge, and a public car park can be found on the left. Almost opposite, there is a Thames Path Walk to Mapledurham that takes you past *Hardwick Hall* in Whitchurch, (a walk of about a mile and a half) the home of Tom, Philip and Caroline Powys. The house is on the other side of the river but can be clearly seen. Cassandra Leigh (Mrs Austen) almost certainly visited the Powys family here many times. (The walk continues to Mapledurham – a further mile and a half – but it is not necessary, unless you are keen of course, to walk this far as the connection is so tenuous, (it concerns Alexander Pope) although the Leighs may have visited; the Powys family certainly did.

Having completed your walk, return to the roundabout, and turn right. A short distance to a T-junction and turn right again. (There is another car park on the left before the railway bridge, and can be used if the other car park has too many restrictions.) You will pass a fine view of the Thames on your right, then Child Beale Trust and then traffic lights. Shortly after traffic lights and a bridge over the railway, you reach *Basildon Park* on the left. This has connections with <u>Warren Hastings</u>. Sir Francis Sykes, the builder-owner of Basildon Park, returned from India with Warren Hastings' son and handed the child over to George Austen. *Pride and Prejudice*, starring Keira Knightley and Ian McFadden, was filmed here when Basildon Park became Netherfield. The house was also used for a picnic scene in a BBC2 production to commemorate the 200th anniversary of Jane's death. This is the end of this excursion and you may like to reward yourself by patronising the Basildon Park café before or after touring the house. Basildon Park was completely refurbished by new owners in the early twentieth century so is not the original that Warren Hastings would have visited.

Obviously, there is a need for transport on all three of these excursions. There is, of course, a fourth option: take a cruise along the River Thames, stopping off where convenient.

Henley-on-Thames and Harpsden

Synopsis

Nestled in the Oxfordshire hills, overlooking the river, half-way between Henley and Shiplake, sits the tiny village of Harpsden. The Reverend Thomas Leigh, Jane Austen's grandfather, was rector of Harpsden from 1731 to 1764 and that is where his children were born – including Jane Austen's mother Cassandra.

In Oxford, it was Theophilus Leigh, Master of Baliol, who, despite his small stature was seen as the academic, aristocratic personage, a colourful character, a shining light in Oxford academia. He was also probably a little bit of an eccentric. <u>Thomas Leigh</u> of Harpsden, brother of Theophilus (and William who was the Cooke of Bookham connection), was known as 'chick' Leigh. This was not so much because of his handsome face, but because he looked, and was, so young: he was sixteen when he entered Christ Church. He was born at Adlestrop – a village that was to become well-known to Jane Austen. Thomas Leigh has been described as a contented, quiet, sweet-tempered, generous and cheerful man. When he became rector of Harpsden in 1731, he married <u>Jane Walker</u> who brought a pedigree to the union to equal her husband's, an acerbic tongue too by some accounts. This maternal grandmother of Jane Austen could boast amongst her ancestry, a Lord Mayor of London in 1553 and the founder (Sir Thomas White who will be mentioned in Reading) of St John's College, Oxford. One cannot help feeling that Jane Austen would have loved her grandfather but she may have placed her grandmother in the same category as her Leigh-Perrot aunt. However, both of these grandparents had died before she was born. Jane Walker's mother was Jane Perrot whose family inheritance enabled Jane's uncle James Leigh, to build Scarlets and to enjoy a growing fortune.

Harpsden now (up) and then (down)

Although now embracing the Church of England faith, there were many of the Leigh family (including Theophilus) who remained loyal to the 'old' (Roman Catholic) religion. There were other families in similar circumstances, especially in this part of the Thames valley. In an England of a small population, comparatively speaking, it was not surprising that those families knew, or knew of each other. They would have met in London, in Bath, in Oxford, in the Midlands. When Thomas and Jane Leigh began their married life in Harpsden, there would have been a ready-made society for them to enter, to entertain and be entertained by – the Powys family being the most likely of these (they owned property near the Leighs of Stoneleigh Abbey) or perhaps the Blounts of Mapledurham and the family at Stonor Park.

The River Thames cannot be seen from Harpsden, nor even from the Reading Road at this point today. Although there were wooded areas in this part of the Thames valley in Jane's day, it would nevertheless have been more open and glimpses of the river more forthcoming then.

James Leigh was born and baptised in 1735 in Harpsden. He later became James Leigh-Perrot whom we will meet in Hare Hatch and Wargrave. Jane Leigh, born in 1736, was the beauty of the family and was the mother of Jane Cooper, a school friend and close companion of the Austen girls. Cassandra, Jane Austen's mother, was born in 1739. It seems that Cassandra inherited her mother's acerbic tongue but the wit and intelligence from the Leighs. Perhaps her father's laid-back approach to life too, explains her willingness to live a quiet modus vivendi in Hampshire. The youngest child had learning difficulties and moved to Steventon with his mother in her old age, she was to live with the Austens and he, probably, where the Austen's own son, George boarded.

Of all the friendships of the Leigh family, it was the Coopers and the Powys families who became closest to Jane's mother, Cassandra Leigh and the three families became intertwined through marriage. The Coopers lived at Phyllis Court – owned by Gislington Cooper – a country estate with its landscaped grounds sweeping down to the River Thames. It became the centre of Henley's social scene before the Coopers sold it when Gislington Cooper died. The Leighs of Harpsden would have been amongst their guests as sure as the Bennets were at Netherfield in *Pride and Prejudice*. And who knows, perhaps a few years later, George Austen was a guest too, taken along by his college friend, Tom Powys or William East. The house was demolished in 1837 and another was rebuilt, now it is a private members club. The grounds, however, still hold a Georgian charm and Jane Austen and the Leighs would be familiar with the view that it continues to command up and down the River Thames.

When the children grew up, romance blossomed, for Cassandra's beautiful sister Jane married Edward Cooper from Phyllis Court, who was to eventually become vicar of Sonning. Edward's sister Ann Cooper married Ralph Cawley (Rector of Stepney; there were Cawleys living in Henley) in April 1768, two months after the death of her father. She was the lady who tutored the Austen sisters and Edward Cooper's daughter, Jane, in Oxford and Southampton. Another young lady who remained a close family friend for the rest of her life was Mary Newell of Henley Park (the property of Gislington Cooper) who later became Mrs George Birch and moved to a house in Windsor. She was a favourite of Jane Austen who visited her there at least twice.

August and September 1799 saw several members of the Austen family visiting Edward and Caroline Cooper, no doubt because the young couple were about to depart for Hamstall Ridware, and this might be the last opportunity to visit Cassandra's childhood home. The visitors were George Austen, his wife Cassandra, his son and daughter-in-law James and Mary Austen and his two daughters Cassandra and Jane Austen. We know this from the diaries of Caroline Powys but it is not clear how long the Austen family stayed in Harpsden and if all of them were there at the same time. There is no clue from any source to hint that any of them visited the Leigh-Perrots at Scarlets although that couple could have been in Bath at the time. George Austen possessed his own carriage in 1797 and it would be nice [Oh dear, Henry Tilney would tick me off for using that word] to think that the Austens travelled in their own equipage to Harpsden in 1799. However, some writers suggest that he ceased using it in 1798 when William Pitt introduced yet another new tax. The Austen ladies probably travelled post.

There were other visits to Henley. Henry and Jane were there as late as May 1813 as can be seen from her letter to Cassandra when she asked for good weather. According to Jane's letters, Henry Austen travelled several times to Oxfordshire. In 1796, he stopped off on his way to his Master's degree in Oxford and in March 1798 he was longer in the town when he had been transferred to Henley to help in the training of new recruits, over 350 of whom were added to his regiment. Only once does Jane specify Henley when she herself accompanied him via Windsor. It is evident from letters that Henry was in the habit of calling in at Harpsden on the way to Oxford and his duties, when in the militia, also took him to Henley. In 1801, when Henry resigned from the Oxford militia, he set up as an army agent for distributing money to regiments. Sometime in 1806, he established the bank of Austen, Maunde & Austen (Later Austen, Maunde and Tilson) in London, still with contacts in Oxfordshire. Perhaps Henry had a banking business to attend to when he and Jane visited Henley in 1813. However, the date may be significant. In 1813, Henry was appointed Receiver-General of land and assessed taxes for Oxfordshire. Also, according to Jane, Henry made his first peripatetic collection in September. On the 16th of that month, Henry proposed to meet Cassandra at Bagshot and take her into Oxfordshire. Did Cassandra also visit Henley that year or did Henry take her to, presumably Henley, by another route? Interestingly, the A321 begins at Henley then passes through Wargrave, Twyford, Wokingham, Sandhurst and then, at Blackwater joins the A30 with a left turning to Bagshot. A (arterial) road did not exist as such in those days of course, but they are based on the major, well-established, routes of the past. Henry also visited Mrs Crutchley (a widow and a prospective second wife for him) at Sunning Hill which is on the A329 that joins the A321 at Wokingham. On the Berkshire side of the Henley bridge, Jane – and any of her people – travelling between Windsor or Maidenhead and Henley would have enjoyed a safer road which climbed out of Henley as White's Hill. This dangerously steep hill, especially at the bottom as it approached the bridge, had been made safer by no less a personage than Thomas Gainsborough's brother, Humphrey, an Independent minister living in Henley where he used the engineering skills that he had developed, on roads and bridges in the area. Having travelled down the hill out of Berkshire and across the bridge into Oxfordshire, there were inns on either side: the Angel on the left and on the right the more salubrious, Red Lion. When Henry and Jane visited Henley, after their relations and friends had departed the area, did they stop at the Red Lion for refreshment or for fresh horses? This inn was famous for its mutton chops. The Prince Regent (later George IV) enjoyed Mrs Dixon's chops. He was often in Henley visiting local landowners. Jane Austen would have been thrilled to learn that both Dr Johnson and James Boswell had visited the inn.

Connections between Jane Austen and Henley-on-Thames dwindled when James Leigh Perrot died. Later, long after James had died and his nephew James Edward came to live at Scarlets, the family became more involved with local events until he eventually left to take up his appointment in Bray. However, no doubt when his son became vicar of Wargrave Arthur Henry Austen Leigh would have visited this town for shopping, for leisure and for official occasions. Henley Regatta which was established in 1839 would have been one attraction that drew the Austen-Leighs to the town and as late as 1873 the event saw other generations attend it. Interestingly both Jane's tutors – Mrs Cawley and Mrs La Tournelle – are buried in Henley.

Supporting Evidence

William Shenstone (1714–1763) lines written on a pane in one of the Red Lion Inn windows:

Whoe'er has travelled life's dull round
Where'er his stages may have been
May sigh to think that he has found
His warmest welcome at an inn.

(*There is no evidence that Shenstone carved his own words on the window. They could have been etched there at a much later date. Jane and Henry Austen may have seen them. The poem no longer exists in situ as the inn has undergone considerable and many changes and extensions over the years*)

Reading Mercury 1767

If the hill could be rendered less steep, and consequently more safe, at a moderate expense, by removing some of the ground at the top of the hill and laying it at the bottom as has lately been done at Henley-on-Thames it would be desirable.

Horace Walpole visiting his friend at Remenham a village on the river opposite Henley [Describes the area as] Not a sight on the island more worthy of being visited.

From the Diaries of Mrs Philip Lybbe Powys in 1789

We all went to tea at Mr Cooper's at Henley to see the illuminations [fireworks] at Henley town on the King's recovery [George III]. Every house was lighted up, and as we walked about for hours different parties from the neighbourhood [did this include the Leigh-Perrots from Scarlets, the Easts from Hurley, the Coopers from Sonning?]

the whole made a very fine sight. Fawley Court [Caroline and Philip Lybbe Powys were now living at Fawley rectory] looked vastly well from the bridge.

From the Diaries of Mrs Philip Lybbe Powys 27 October 1794

Our dear Caroline brought to bed of a son [at Harpsden]

And 3 December

Edward Philip Cooper was christened at Harpsden Church [the father then curated there]. My mother, Mr Powys, Mrs Williams [Jane Cooper] Henry Austen, sponsors.

(*Sponsors did not necessarily attend the ceremony, but this may have been another instance when Henry stayed at Harpsden or Henley*)

Jane Austen's Letters: letter 1 to Cassandra from Steventon 9–10 January 1796
… Henry goes to Harden [Harpsden] today in his way to his Master's degree [at Oxford]

Jane Austen's Letters: Letter 2 to Cassandra from Steventon 14–15 January 1796

… I wrote principally to tell you that the Coopers were arrived and in good health – the little boy is very like Dr Cooper & the little girl is to resemble Jane, they say.

Reading Mercury 21 March 1796

HENLEY-UPON-THAMES, OXON

MRS LA TOURNELL

Having been enabled by the generosity liberality of her friendship to succeed MRS DARBY in her SCHOOL in BELL STREET, takes this method of returning them her most grateful thanks, and requests the continuance of their patronage to complete her re-establishment. She humbly flatters herself that her conduct in that line, for upwards of thirty years in the FORBURY, READING, will induce the public to repost full confidence in her.

NB THE SCHOOL OPENS, on Mrs La Tournelle's account, after the Easter week.

The Diary of Mrs Philip Lybbe Powys 7 July 1797

Casandra Louisa's christening at Harpsden Church. Mrs Austen and my daughter Louisa godmothers. Dr Ishim godfather

(*This does not mean that Mrs Austen was actually in attendance, although she may have visited with some of her family – Cassandra and Jane, for instance*)

Letter 12 to Cassandra from Steventon 25 November 1798

By the bye, I have written to Mrs Birch [Mrs Austen's friend Mary Newell] among my other writings and so hope to have some account of all the people in that part of the world [Windsor] before long.

Letter 18 to Cassandra from Steventon 21–23 January 1799

…Yesterday came a letter to my mother from Edward Cooper to announce, not the birth of a child, but of a living; for Mrs Leigh has begged his acceptance of the Rectory of Hamstall-Ridware in Staffordshire, vacant by Mr Johnson's death. We collect from his letter that he means to reside there, in which he shows his wisdom. Staffordshire is a good way off; so we shall see nothing of them till, some fifteen years hence, the Miss Coopers are presented to us, fine, jolly, handsome, ignorant girls. The living is valued at *l*40 [£40] a year, but perhaps it may be improvable. How will they be able to convey the furniture of the dressing-room so far in safety?

(*The fact that Jane is familiar with the furniture at the Rectory of Harpsden, suggests that she has already made at least one visit there. One wonders if she also called in to see her uncle and aunt at Scarlets although, as ever, they may have been in Bath at the time.*)

Letter 21 to Cassandra from 13 Queen Square 11 June 1799

…I wonder what we shall do with our intended visits this summer? I should like to make a compromise with Adlestrop, Harden [Harpsden] & Bookham – that Martha's spending the summer at Steventon should be considered as our respective visits to them all.

The Diary of Mrs Philip Lybbe Powys August 12 1799

… we took Miss Pringle to Harpsden to stay at Coopers til they returned. Mr Mrs and Mr James Austen were there.

(w*here were Jane and Cassandra?*)

The Diary of Mrs Philip Lybbe Powys 13 September 1799

...was to me one of the most melancholy days I ever experienced, as it was to part me and my dearest Caroline, who was to set off the next day for Staffordshire; and as Mr Cooper was to do duty at Henley Church that day for Mr Townsend, he thought it best they should all lay at Henley, [at the Red Lion or Mr Townsend's rectory behind it?] to make the separation less dismal.

(*Mrs Powys would later comment upon the excellent preaching of her son-in-law which was already showing signs of evangelical much to Jane's disgust*)

Letter 85 to Cassandra from Sloane Street 20 May 1813

... get us the best weather you can for Wednesday, Thursday & Friday. We are to go to Windsor [to visit Mrs Birch?] in our way to Henley, which will be a great delight ... I should not wonder if we got no farther than Reading on Thursday evening & so reach Steventon only to a reasonable Dinner hour the next day.

Letters from Mrs Mary Birch to her children 5 February 1836

My Dearest General,

...Then after reading prayers to my family, a chapter in the testament, and private prayers myself, eat a good breakfast, and sat in anxious expectation for Mr & Mrs Cooper and their two little girls who had sent me word they would call in on their way to Essex, where they were going; not having seen them for four years, their visit was a matter of real interest, as they were the 6th generation of two families which I had known intimately.

And 4th September 1836

My Dearest John,

…She also sent me word yesterday that she had heard from Mr Powys's niece (Charlotte Powys) that Mr Powys had recovered his speech…She told me that Edward Cooper had the living of Burford and Philip Cooper a small living themselves…

(*Mrs Birch also reminisces about the Hunt at Stonor*)

June 1873 diary of Emma Casandra Leigh, daughter of J.E.A.L.

[went to Windsor Park to see the] Great Review given in honour of the Shah of Persia [the next day] went to Henley Regatta with the Chilton's and [members of the Leigh Family listed.]

Phyllis Court and Fawley

Synopsis

Phyllis Court was owned and lived in by Gislington Cooper until his death in 1768; he also owned Henley Park. He was a banker and goldsmith of St Clements Dane, London. As I have said, perhaps George Austen accompanied his friends to Phyllis Court sometimes and although I understand that they met in Bath (or Oxford) and married there too, I do wonder if he danced with his future wife in Henley. Perhaps this is where Caroline Girle, living in Caversham at the time, danced with Philip Lybbe Powys, having met him at a Reading or Henley Assembly.

This was the era when Bath was growing in fashionable popularity so it would be natural for these families to follow the vogue. We have seen that the Leigh-Perrots bought a house and stayed regularly in Bath until James's death, and the Edward Coopers went there too. And we mustn't forget that this was where George Austen married Cassandra Leigh, the ceremony performed by their good friend Tom Powys at Walcot church. We should not be surprised that George Austen chose to spend the last years of his life in a place where happy, youthful memories abound.

The 1760s were an important crossroads for Cassandra Leigh. Her father retired to Bath in 1764 and died that same year. Cassandra married George Austen shortly afterwards in that same city. By the end of the decade, Cassandra's brother James was living at Scarlets and sister Jane married, in 1768, Dr Edward Cooper, first living between London and Southcote on the other side of Reading. Cassandra herself moved completely out of the areas of both Henley and Bath to live with her husband in Deane and then Steventon in Hampshire. It was the end of Leigh's residency in Henley although James and his wife perhaps visited the town from time to time, possibly to attend a ball, play with 'fish' at a card party or enjoy dinner at one of the country houses where he still knew the residents. He would especially be pleased to join in the local hunt held at the Henley estates and may have joined in Henley celebrations. Phyllis Court was sold in 1768 after the death of Gislington Cooper. Precipitating, probably, the marriage of the two children: Edward to Jane Leigh and Anne to Ralph Cawley. It was a pity that Jane Austen never visited Phyllis Court. "Queen Anne, the Consort of James I visited the manor in 1604 and in 1643, Oliver Cromwell built the wall that still edges the garden where it fronts the Thames. Just forty-five years later, William of Orange held his first court here, on his way to London." (Phyllis Court Club brochure) Jane, with her pithy wit, would surely have had something interesting to say about all of that. It was in the village of Fawley that Tom Powys was presented with a living on 30 October 1762 by Sambrook Freeman of Fawley Court.

St Mary's Church at Fawley

The living was later given to his nephew and namesake Thomas, younger son of Philip Lybbe and Caroline Powys. Philip and Caroline (Girle) Powys began their married life in Whitchurch but as they grew older handed over the estate to their eldest son. They then went to live in Fawley, where Brother Tom Powys held a living which he held onto whilst Deane of Canterbury. It is possible that Mrs Austen visited her friend Caroline at Fawley or even visited Fawley church, to see her friend Tom in the remaining two years when she was living in Harpsden. If she had, she would have been particularly interested in the church chancel. Her grandfather, Theophilus Leigh of Adlestrop married, as his second wife and Cassandra's grandmother, the Hon Mary Brydges who was the eldest daughter of Sir James Brydges, eighth Lord Chandos of Sudely. She was also the sister of James Brydges, the first Duke of Chandos. It was this ostentatious brother of Mary Leigh who lived in his splendid mansion near Edgware which he called 'Cannons'. In 1748, John Freeman, the current owner of Fawley Court rebuilt the chancel of the church using fittings from 'Cannons'. It was from this branch of the family that the name Cassandra originates, Cassandra Willoughby having married the first Duke.

When Mrs Austen and her two daughters visited the Coopers (young Edward now curated at Harpsden, and his the curate, the daughter of the Philip and Caroline Powys), there was a natural reunion between the two friends. On one occasion in 1799, Caroline Powys recorded in her diary that she entertained the Misses <u>Cassandra and Jane Austen</u> to dinner at Fawley. When Philip Powys died, Caroline went to live in New Street, Henley. Meanwhile, their son Thomas died, and Caroline went to Fawley to commiserate with her daughter-in-law who had been left with eleven children under seventeen, but herself died there. All of the Powys family were buried in Whitchurch.

It is not necessary to travel further along the Marlow Road but it is worth remembering the wicked Sir Francis Dashwood of the infamous Hellfire Club at Medmenham. There is a connection between this man and Thomas Knight, who adopted Jane Austen's brother Edward. Francis Dashwood and Thomas Knight knew each other well. Did this influence Jane's choice of the Dashwood name in *Sense and Sensibility*?

Supporting evidence

The Diary of Mrs Philip Lybbe Powys 1784
We came to reside with my brother at Fawley, August the 10th, as we found Hardwick too large for only Mr Powys,

myself and Caroline, after being used to so large a family … but as the situation of Fawley is likewise delightful, and the house, tho small, compact and elegant, it had ever been a favourite place with us all, and of course we removed with less regret as it in many respects was certainly much more eligible.

(*The eldest son, Philip Powys, moved into Hardwick House with his growing family*)

The Diary of Mrs Philip Lybbe Powys 21 July 1791

Miss Cooper [Austen's cousin Jane] came for a week, and we went [from Fawley] on the 22 a large party, to Clifden Spring by water, towed [by horse on the towpath?] there and back in Mr Freeman's new boat, a very elegant one.

The Diary of Mrs Philip Lybbe Powys 2 September 1799

[Fawley] The Coopers to Dinner and with them the two Miss Austens and Mr W Warren.

Hurley

Synopsis

Hall Place

On high ground, above and beyond the village of Hurley, is a mansion known as Hall Place. The estate was purchased in 1728 by the young, wealthy London lawyer William East. He demolished the old Hall and built the present mansion. He was succeeded by his posthumous son who became Sir William East, a university friend of George Austen. Sir William's son, Gilbert, was one of George Austen's four pupils at Steventon joining his sons Edward and Henry. Perhaps the recommendation came from the Leigh-Perrot near-neighbours or maybe Gilbert became Mr Austen's pupil because of his father being at university with him. Probably a bit of both. Gilbert was the subject of some verses which were written by Mrs Austen during the long absence of the society-loving boy. Sir William was a keen apiarist and no doubt sent jars of honey to the Austens each time Gilbert went to Steventon, although the Austens had their own beehives (daughter Cassandra became a keen apiarist) and no doubt reciprocated with their own gift of honey. When Gilbert finished his education under George Austen, Sir William presented his friend with a picture, which seems to have been a portrait, in appreciation.

Gilbert East succeeded his father but he died childless and the baronetcy became extinct. The estate was inherited by Gilbert's nephew George Clayton who adopted the name East. The family continued in this ownership until 1939 when Hall Place was requisitioned by the government. The estate was sold in 1948 to the Ministry of Agriculture and established as the Berkshire Institute of Agriculture in 1949, now the Berkshire College of Agriculture. Since 1948 there has been a substantial programme of restoration, extension and development and efforts have been made to preserve the character of Hall Place, while fulfilling the educational needs and requirements of the College. The preservation of two original chimney pieces are a particular achievement.

In St Mary the Virgin church, which stands on the banks of the River Thames in the actual village, there are many commemorations to Sir William and his family.

SIR W? EAST.
Late of Hallplace
Bart. did by his Will.
dated April. 23? 1815.
give to Trustees
Twelve London Af-
-surance Shares, in
Trust to pay the an-
-nual profits thereof
to a poor Man, and
his Wife. Parishioners
of and resident in
the parish of Hurley
but not receiving
support from the
Parish to be nom-
-inated by the owner
for the Time being of
Hallplace.

SACRED
TO THE MEMORY OF
SIR GILBERT EAST.
OF HALL PLACE
IN THE COUNTY OF BERKS BART
WHO WAS BORN 17? APRIL 1764.
DIED 11? DECEMBER 1828.

When she passed the village of Hurley, (which she would have done travelling between Windsor and Henley) Jane may have given a shudder if she knew of the connections with Lady Place (next to the church). John, third Lord Lovelace of Hurley, used the monks' crypt at Lady Place to plot secretly the deposition of the Stuart king, James II. An inscription used to be found declaring, 'In this place, the Revolution of 1688 was begun.' However, perhaps her love affair with the Stuarts, with whom she sympathised in the margin of her history textbook, came to an end after Charles I, although she excuses herself for this by writing that her aim in writing her *History* had been to prove the innocence of Mary Queen of Scots and to vilify Elizabeth I. We shall never know for her *History of England* ended with this beheaded, 'betrayed' sovereign.

There is another interesting remote connection with Hurley that Jane Austen may or may not have known about. Richard Lovelace, the poet, was closely related to the Lovelace of Lady Place (His *Lucasta going to the Wars* was dedicated to Lady Ann of Hurley). Harris Bigg Wither was a descendant of the poet.

The vicar of Hurley during the time when Jane Austen's family and connections lived in the area was William Fordyce Mavor (1789–1838) The Rev Mavor invented a system of shorthand, published in 1779. He wrote forty books including *A General View of Agriculture in Berkshire*, extracts of which give an insight of the Berkshire that Jane knew. He was perhaps another member of the Leigh Perrot literary circle.

Supporting evidence

To Lucasta, going to the War by Richard Lovelace 1640
   Tell me not (sweet) I am unkind
   That from the nunnery
   Of thy chaste breast and quiet mind
   To war and arms I fly…

   (*Dedicated to Lady Ann of Hurley*)

The Diary of Mrs Philip Lybbe Powys 11 October 1776
   From my brother's [Thomas Powys] at Fawley we went to see Hurley Priory, Berks, an immense old white house. Formerly it belonged to Lord Lovelace but now is in possession of Mr Wilcox … the cellars of this house have long been famous for their goodness, tho' they are uncommonly so, but because in them was planned the Revolution. The servant informed us two kings had dined there … The following inscription is placed against a wall: Be it remembered that the Revolution of 1688 was begun …

   (*The plaque existed until 1831*)

Collected Poems and Verse of the Austen Family ed David Selwyn
   First verse written by Mrs Austen:
   Your Steventon Friends
   Are at their wits' ends
   To know what has become of Squire East;
   They very much fear
   He'll never come here

Having left them nine weeks at the least.

Notes in the margin of Jane Austen's copy of Goldsmith's 'History of England'

... always ill-used, BETRAYED AND NEGLECTED

... Oh! The Wretches [alluding to the Cromwellians]

Letter 29 to Cassandra from Steventon 3–5 January 1801

... as to our pictures, the Battle piece, Mr Nibbs, Sir Wm East, all the old heterogenous miscellany, manuscripts, Scriptorial pieces dispersed over the House are to be given to James.

(*Mr & Mrs Austen, Cassandra, and Jane were on the point of moving to Bath. They would lodge with the Leigh-Perrots until such time as they found a house of their own to rent.*)

Wargrave

Synopsis

Hare Hatch, where Scarlets stands, is in the parish of Wargrave where our interest mainly lies at this moment. When <u>James Leigh Perrot</u> died in 1817, the funeral took place in Wargrave and he is buried in the churchyard there.

Both James and Jane Leigh Perrot are buried here

The <u>Austen brothers</u> attended the funeral. Cassandra Austen went to Scarlets to comfort her aunt. Almost certainly there would have been a plaque to commemorate James Leigh

Perrot mounted on the wall inside the church, but as this church was burned to the ground by suffragettes a century later, it is no longer to be seen. Jane Leigh Perrot is also buried here. A survivor in life, it seems that she was also a survivor of sorts in death as hers was the only plaque which did escape destruction in the fire and can still be seen in the church today.

Mrs Jane Leigh Perrot's plaque is still to be seen in the church at Wargrave

In addition to our interest in the church, we must add a list of names that are in some way connected with Jane Austen. Wargrave remains full of houses that were known to the Leigh Perrots and can easily evoke a sense of the time in which we are interested. Joseph Hill lived in the village. Jane Austen was acquainted with this lawyer who was the man of affairs for the branch of the Leigh family to which Jane's mother belonged. Not only was Hill a neighbour and friend of James Leigh-Perrott, but Austen and Hill were both guests together at Stoneleigh Abbey in August 1806. Mrs Austen and her two daughters had been visiting her cousin Thomas Leigh at Adlestrop when he received news from Hill that the owner, Mary Leigh, had died. Hill advised an immediate visit to Stoneleigh as the inheritance, ostensibly Thomas's, could be in dispute. Mrs Austen had her own interest as it was likely that her brother James Leigh-Perrot could also have a claim. So, off they all went: Thomas Leigh, Mrs Austen, Cassandra, Jane and Joseph Hill. When she was 'lopping and cropping' *Pride and Prejudice*, one must wonder if Jane Austen remembered this diligent lawyer when naming the Bennets' family housekeeper – "Hill, where's Hill?" calls Mrs Bennet in the 1995 television production of that book. Joseph Hill was a lifelong friend of the poet Cowper who was known to be admired by Jane Austen and quoted in most of her novels. In November 1784, Cowper published *The Task*, a favourite poem of Austen's (and Fanny's in *Mansfield Park*). Included in this publication, Cowper addressed his friend and benefactor in *An Epistle to Joseph Hill*. No doubt, when they dined at Stoneleigh, Jane would have been fascinated to hear any news of Joseph Hill's friend William Cowper.

Another resident of Wargrave was the mother of Thomas Day, author and member of the Lunar Society. Day met his death in Wargrave when riding to visit his mother and is buried in the churchyard there. He is best remembered for his book *The History of Sandford and Merton* (1783–89) which was almost certainly known to George Austen who may have owned a copy. The story is about two boys being educated by a pastor. Like William Cowper, Day was a fervent abolitionist – a subject skirted in *Mansfield Park*. In 1773 Day co-published a long poem *The Dying Negro*. Day was a friend of Richard Edgeworth (whom we will meet at Scarlets).

Richard Barry, 7th Earl of Barrymore, also knew Wargrave. He was a prankster, gambler, sportsman, sexual predator, friend of the future George IV and keen on the theatre. The family was almost as notorious as he was. One of his flights of fancy was to build a theatre in Wargrave – a costly enterprise where he directed and acted in plays that he presented there. The Powys family certainly went to see some of the plays and it was likely that the Leigh Perrots did too.

Arthur Henry Austen Leigh, son of James Edward, aged one when he first came to live at Scarlets, became vicar of Wargrave in 1890 and his grave is to be found in the churchyard. His sister, Mary Augusta was the first Austen Leigh child to be born at Scarlets and spoke of a visit by Cassandra Leigh.

Supporting evidence

Extract from 'An Epistle to Joseph Hill' published by William Cowper in November 1784

> Some few that I have known in days of old
> Would run most dreadful risk of catching cold
> While you, my friend, whatever wind should blow
> Might traverse England safely to and fro.
> An honest man, close-buttoned to the chin
> Broadcloth without and a warm heart within.

The Diary of Mrs Philip Lybbe Powys January 31 1788

> Lord Barrymore had the last summer built a very elegant playhouse at Wargrave, had a Mr Young from the Opera House to paint the scenes, which were extremely pretty. His

Lordship and friends performed three nights one week. We were all there the 31st. It was extremely full of the neighbouring families. The play was *The Confederacy* and *The Midnight Hour*.

(*also attended in August 1789 and September 21 1790*)

Epitaph in St Mary's Church, Wargrave (destroyed in the fire by suffragettes)

In memory of Thomas Day Esq
Who died on 27 Sept 1789
Aged 41
After having promoted by the Energy of his Writings
And encouraged by the Uniformity of his Example
The unremitted exercise of
Every public and private
Virtue

Extract from 'Mansfield Park' ch vi published 1814

Fanny, who was sitting on the other side of Edmund, exactly opposite Miss Crawford, and who had been attentively listening, now looked at him, and said in a low voice, 'Cut down an avenue! What a pity! Does not it make you think of Cowper? "Ye fallen avenues, once more I mourn your fate unmerited".'

Plaque on the West Wall of St Mary's church, Wargrave

Jane
Daughter of
Robert Cholmeley Esq

And widow of
James Leigh Perrot Esq
Died at Scarlets in this parish
Nov 13th 1836 aged 92
In humble hope that through the merits
Of her redeemer she shall rejoin
In heaven, him who had been the object
Of her constant and undiminished
Affection upon earth
Through fifty years of wedlock,
And twenty of widowhood.

(*one must wonder if Jane Leigh Perrot composed her own epitaph*)

Short Biography of J.E.A.L by Mary Augusta Austen Leigh

[Cassandra was] a pale, dark-eyed old lady, with a high arched nose and a kind smile, dressed in a long cloak and a large drawn bonnet, both made of black satin. She looked to me quite different from anyone I had ever seen.

from the JAS Report 1999 – an article by Hazel Jones.

Scarlets, Hare Hatch

Synopsis

Scarlets is a substantial house (rescued from dereliction in the 1970s and now divided into three private residences), situated in Scarlets Lane just off the Bath Road – the A4. In the sixteenth century, the property passed to the Spiers family and from them to the Perrots of North Leigh in Oxfordshire. James Leigh, Mrs Austen's brother, was connected with this family through their father, Reverend Thomas Leigh, who married Jane Walker, a descendant of the Spiers and Perrots (referred to in Harpsden). When he inherited Northleigh, James added Perrot to his name – becoming <u>James Leigh-Perrot</u> – sold his property to the Duke of Marlborough and built the smaller house, Scarlets in 1764. He married Jane Cholmeley who was born in Barbados. She left for school in England at the age of six years old. If Jane Austen knew this, it may have had a bearing on her disparaging remarks about children being sent off to certain boarding schools, comparing them unfavourably with that of Mrs Goddard (*Emma*).

The life of the Leigh-Perrots was a privileged one. A remark that Mrs Leigh-Perrot once made after her husband James's death, remembering living in style 'dining with thirty families', (possibly an off-spoken boast) reminds us of an incident in *Pride and Prejudice* when the Bingley sisters are derisive of Mrs Bennet's boast of entertaining twenty-four families at one sitting. They were a sociable couple and when not in Bath, attended local events in Henley and Reading as well as being entertained by other local well-to-do families.

Jane-Leigh Perrot may have been unpopular with Jane Austen but her husband was a devoted spouse loving her until the end of his days. However, despite her dislike of the woman, when her uncle died, making light of her own illness, Jane insisted that her sister Cassandra should go to Scarlets to assist their aunt. Jane's eldest brother James visited Scarlets several times (expecting to inherit) and was probably delighted to join in the local hunt.

Jane Leigh-Perrot had connections through her favourite niece, with George Crabbe, another poet admired by Austen. In *Mansfield Park*, Crabbe's *Tale in Verse* was amongst the books owned by Fanny Price. J W Chapman speculates that Austen 'probably had some sort of introduction to Maria Edgeworth; without it, she would hardly have sent her a presentation copy of *Emma*'. Did the Leigh-Perrots perform this courtesy? However, did Jane Austen actually sanction the sending of the copy? She was annoyed that Murray (her publisher) had dispersed copies of *Emma,* leaving her without one for her youngest brother Charles. Although Maria lived mostly in Ireland, the Edgeworths had become neighbours of the Leigh-Perrots when Mr Edgeworth moved to the area in 1766. Maria was born in 1768 whilst the family still lived at Hare Hatch although a different source gives her birthplace in Oxfordshire, perhaps because she was baptised in the parish church where the Edgeworth had previously lived. Friendship ensued and James Leigh-Perrot helped with Richard Edgeworth's scientific experiments, which included telegraphing from Hare Hatch to Nettlebed by means of windmills. Like Thomas Day, Edgeworth was a member of the Lunar Society.

The Leigh Perrots spent their time between Scarlets and Bath. No doubt it began with fashion and affection for the city but they no doubt went there also due to James's health. He took the waters for his gout. Many people are uncomfortable with ill health, especially in others, and develop a feeling of inadequacy when unable to help with the relief of the symptoms; impatience develops. The Leighs are an interesting case when comparing their longevity (witness Theophilus Leigh and Francis Austen) with James Leigh-Perrot, James Austen, Edward Austen, Henry Austen, James Edward Austen Leigh, Jane Austen, even Edward Cooper and, of course, Mrs George Austen all of whom we learn had health problems from time to time. Was Jane impatient with her mother because she lived with it all the time? Because she felt inadequate? Because mothers are not expected to be ill?

When the Leigh-Perrots were undergoing a period of stress and hardship in Bath (Jane had been arrested for supposedly stealing some lace), Mr Edgeworth wrote a letter of support. He said that he had known the Leigh-Perrots for over thirty-four years and remembered them for their decency. Mrs Austen offered the companionship of Cassandra and Jane but Mrs Leigh-Perrot said that where she was 'imprisoned' was no place for genteel girls. Fortunately, after consideration which lasted for less than ten minutes, the jurors returned a verdict of 'not guilty' and Mrs Leigh-Perrot was released.

It is clear that the Leigh-Perrots had many literary connections which Jane Austen would have been keen to hear about. She often saw her uncle (of whom she was very fond) and aunt (whom she did not like very much at all) in Bath and could glean such news about these creative people or of them, either there in Bath, when they visited them at Steventon or in the letters that were regularly exchanged between the Leighs and the Austens. After Jane Austen's death, her aunt wrote a letter to James Edward Austen in October 1828. She says of her niece's writing, 'I have been reading *Emma* a second time, but I still cannot like it so well as poor Jane's other novels.' Much of Uncle Leigh-Perrot's wealth was spent on amassing a library. He gave his niece, Jane, a number of expensively bound, multi-volume works.

What a pity that Jane Leigh Perrot was held in such acrimony by Jane Austen. Men are capable of deep passions. The soldier can perform extreme bravery to the point of death; the chef will create a dish that is perfect of taste in every sense of the word; the lover shows tenderness, sacrifice, generosity and the deepest passion of all. It gives James Leigh Perrot's pen might: 'yours lovingly, wholly' and the eyes conviction: 'a smile which gladdens my heart, that said I was valued'. For James, it meant devotion to a woman to almost a total exclusion of his family. Lucky Jane Cholmeley. But the family saw, not a brother or uncle who deserted them, but a woman who took him away. It did not help Mrs Leigh Perrot's cause when lacking a loving family of her own, she became insecure and selfish.

Because of their attachment to Scarlets, Mr Leigh-Perrot was happy to withdraw claims to the estate of Stoneleigh Abbey in return for £24,000 and an annuity until Mrs Leigh-

Perrot's death of £2,000. As she lived to be ninety-two years old, Jane Leigh Perrot received almost £80,000 from the estate.

James Leigh Perrot died in March 1817, leaving everything to his wife – which devastated his sister, Mrs Austen and her family. Nevertheless, Cassandra Austen travelled to Scarlets to support her aunt, closely followed by James, Mary, and Francis. Despite this inherited wealth and perhaps because of the loss incurred by the failure in Henry's bank, Jane Leigh-Perrot felt less secure as a widow and seems to have invested some of her money in the more substantial option of property including cottages from Mr Fonnereau. After James died, his wife used the power of her wealth in a seemingly unsavoury manner. Insecurity manifests itself in many ways. She changed her mind from time to time as to whom should inherit, always keeping the assumed wishes of her dear departed in mind, not to mention the future of her 'pretty Scarlets'. During this time, the Austen men visited Scarlets, no doubt with a view to keeping their inheritance uppermost in their aunt's mind – and wondered why she had never, with the other improvements, planted a thick verge of trees to shut out entirely the road in front of the house. (There is one there now.) Their aunt said that it was because she enjoyed seeing Mr Piggot's cows grazing in the meadow.

Scarlets now hide behind a bank of trees

Jane Leigh-Perrot should not be remembered as a completely selfish and self-centred person, however. It is possible that she bought clothes for her nieces, although reading between the lines of one of Jane's letters, one might think that either Jane did not like her aunt's choice of clothes very much or even that the gown was a castoff. She appeared to resent a gift that could be construed as charity. However, when her father, George Austen, died in Bath, Jane gave credit to the Leigh-Perrots who showed them 'every imaginable kindness'. Neither was her aunt a total skinflint. Having decided to not make Francis Austen her heir after all, she actually gave him, in 1830, £10,000 to buy a house in Portsmouth. She offered 'her dear affectionate sister' Mrs Austen, £100 a year after her son James died (James had been giving his mother an annual allowance of £100). She gave

James's son – James Edward – £300 a year after he obtained his degree and it was this James Edward, Jane Austen's favourite nephew, who finally inherited Scarlets and Mr Leigh Perrot's still considerable fortune.

After his great aunt's death, <u>James Edward Austen Leigh</u> (now commonly referred to as J.E.A.L.) lived at Scarlets until he moved to Bray. When he added 'Leigh' to his name he also took the armorial bearings of Leigh. A royal license was granted to him on 20 January 1837 authorising this and on 6 February the Leigh arms and crest were formally exemplified. A pedigree register of the College of Arms in 1795 shows Cassandra Leigh and her husband the Reverend George Austen with their children, including Jane.

Soon after James Edward and Emma moved into Scarlets, a second daughter was born – Mary Augusta. Four boys arrived afterwards giving them a family of ten children although George died in infancy. This large family triggered various extensions to the house.

James became a local worthy, gradually easing himself into parochial needs as his health improved. (He had problems with his throat.) Soon after his arrival, he was appointed Guardian of the Poor for the Wokingham area and later was a founding member of Reading Hospital Board (Now the Royal Berkshire Hospital). He was partly responsible for Knowle Hill Church (a neighbouring village along the Bath road), the interior of which was painted by Mrs William Smith and his Lefroy cousins. J.E.A.L. became vicar in 1841 and later as Rural Dean hosted meetings at Scarlets (which may have included Gilbert East).

The Austen family continued to visit Scarlets whilst J.E.A.L. was living there of course. In the autumn of 1843,

Cassandra Austen went to stay with her nephew and his family whilst another nephew, Charles, 'began trenching for planting at the back of the cottage gardens in Chawton'.

James Austen-Leigh eventually accepted the Parish of Bray, one of the richest livings in the diocese. Scarlets was finally sold in 1863.

Austen visitors to Scarlets included <u>Mr and Mrs George Austen, James, Edward, Charles, Francis, Cassandra</u> and <u>Mr and Mrs James Edward Austen</u>. But not Jane Austen as far as we know.

Supporting evidence

Letter from Mrs George Austen on 26 August 1770

... had pleasure of leaving my sister [Jane at Southcote, Reading] tolerably well and the child [Edward Cooper] quite so; they are now moved to the country ... we talk of going there and to Scarlets in about three weeks' time and will be absent a full month. I shall take both my boys with me [James and Edward].

Letter from Mrs George Austen 9 December 1770

The Day after Christmas day we are to go to my brother Perrot's for about ten days but then I shall take Neddy as well as Jemmy there being no little ones there to catch anything bad of us.

(*They had been in contact with childhood illnesses*)

From a guide written by Robertson at the end of the Eighteenth century, describing this stretch of the Bath Road.

Pleasingly diversified by farms, cottages and some elegant houses. Bear Place, near Hare Hatch, was the modern residence of Mr Ximenes. Built on rising ground, with open and extensive views towards the south and east, it had replaced a brick and timber house surrounded by a moat. Opposite Bear Place, stood a neat house on a sloping lawn, the residence of Mr James Leigh-Perrot.

The Diary of Mrs Lybbe Powys April 1799

… at a party at Mr Purvis's six tables. Went from thence to a party at Mr Leigh-Perrot's eight tables, ninety people

(This sounds like a card party, the tables accommodated in more than one room. A party of thirty families could mean hosting anything from sixty to ninety or more adults. I cannot imagine hosting so many people in the Scarlets I knew, especially as it had been enlarged at a later date by J.E.A.L. to accommodate his growing family. {My husband and I, together with friends, put in a bid for the dilapidated Scarlets in the 1970s. Our work took my husband and me to Africa, but our four friends went ahead to begin the restoration} We should remember that Jane often complained of a 'sad crush' at some of the local balls to which she went.)

List of guests who during the 1770s–1810s, may have been entertained to dinner or a card party at Scarlets by the Leigh-Perrots.

Mr (later Sir) Morris Ximenes from Bear Place, Hare Hatch

Mrs Day, Mother of Thomas, living at Bear Hill.

Mr and Mrs Pritchard (relatives) living at the Old House (Scarlets estate)

Mr Sheraton from Little Scarlets

The Youngs from Hare Hatch House

Residents of Hare Hatch Grange

Piggot family – Wargrave landowners and local benefactors

Robert Mitchel from Culham Court

Mrs Courthrop, later Lord and Lady Lismore from Castlemaine

Sir William, his wife and Gilbert East, Hurley

Dr Edward Cooper, Jane and Edward jnr of Sonning

Philip and Caroline Powys of Hardwick House and Fawley; children Philip and Thomas

Tom Powys of Fawley

Francis Annesley MP for Reading

George Vansittart MP for Berkshire

Lord Bradbrook

Joseph Hill, family lawyer from Wargrave

Rev Philip Nind Rector of Wargrave living in Hare Hatch

William Stevens, renting Scarlets Farm

Dr James Taylor, a surgeon living at Wargrave House

Rev Mavor, Rector (and prolific author) of Hurley

Mr and Mrs Richard Lovell Edgeworth

Other families from Henley, Fawley, Stonor, Sonning, Wargrave, Remenham, Hurley and Reading. Some will have stayed overnight.

Maria Edgeworth

Thomas Day (wishful thinking!)

William Cowper

(*Most information for this list comes from The Book of*

Wargrave; some are included as known friends of the Leigh Perrots.
Some of the above names can be found in Jane Austen's letters)

Letter from Jane Leigh-Perrot to her cousin whilst awaiting her trial, which took place in 1800.

My dearest Perrot, with his sweet composure adds to my philosophy; to be sure he bids fair to have his patience tried every way he can. Cleanliness has ever been his greatest delight and yet he sees the greasy toast laid by the dirty children on his knees, and feels the small beer trickle down his sleeves on its way across the table unmoved ... Mrs Scudding's knife well licked to clean it from fried onions, helps me now and then – you may believe how the mess I am helped to is disposed of – here are two dogs and three cats always full as hungry as myself.

Letter of support from Mr Edgeworth when Jane Leigh Perrot was arrested

...with tears of indignation in my eyes – aye Sir! With actual, not sentimental tears....

Poem written by James Leigh-Perrot to accompany a gift of some lovely seed pearls to his 'dearest Wife' January 1800

With thee no Days can Winter seem,
Nor Frost, nor Blast can chill;
Thou soft Breeze, the cheering beam,
That keeps in Summer still.
Yours faithfully,
Lovingly and wholly
James Leigh Perrot

Letter 27 to Cassandra from Steventon 20–21 November 1800

Mary said that I looked very well last night; I wore my Aunt's [Mrs Leigh-Perrot] gown & handkerchief, & my hair was at least tidy, which was all my ambition.

Letter 30 to Cassandra 8–9 January 1801

Friday … no answer from my Aunt – she has no time for writing I suppose in the hurry of selling furniture, packing Cloathes & preparing for their removal [from Bath] to Scarlets.

From 'The Parish Register' by George Crabbe

And not one Richard answered to the call …
And Richard Monday at the workhouse sent
There was he punched and pitted, thump'd and fed,
And duly took his beatings and his bread …

(*It is generally thought that Jane took the name Fanny Price from The Parish Register. Was she referring to this Richard when remarking upon Catherine Morland's father's name?*)

Letter 38 to Cassandra from Lyme 14 September 1804

My mother is at this moment reading a letter from my Aunt. Yours to Miss Irvine, of which she had had the perusal (which by the bye, in our place I should not like) – has thrown them into a quandary about Charles & his prospects. The case, is, that my Mother had previously told my Aunt, without restriction, that a sloop (which my Aunt calls a Frigate) was reserved in the East for Charles; whereas you had replied to Miss Irvine's enquiries on the subject with less explicitness & more caution. Never mind, let them puzzle on together. As

Charles will equally go to the E. Indies, my Uncle cannot be really uneasy & my Aunt may do what she likes with her frigates. She talks a great deal of the violent heat of the weather. We know nothing of it here. My Uncle has been suffering a good deal lately; they mean however to go to Scarlets [from Bath] about this time unless prevented by bad accounts of Cook.

Letter 81 to Cassandra from Chawton 9 February 1813

I have letters from my Aunt and from Charles within these few days. My Uncle is quite confined to his Chair by a broken chilblain on one foot and a violent swelling in the other, which my Aunt does not know what to call; there does not seem pain enough for Gout. But you had all this history at Steventon perhaps. She talks of being another fortnight at Scarlets; she is really anxious I can believe to get to Bath as they have an apprehension of their house in Pulteney St. having been broken into.

Letter 86 to Francis Austen from Chawton 3–6 July 1813

… there is another female sufferer on the occasion to be pitied. Poor Mrs L-P who would now have been Mistress of Stoneleigh had there been none of that vile compromise which in good truth has never been allowed to be of much use to them. It will be a hard trial

Letter 87 to Cassandra 15–16 September 1813

I have not yet seen Mr Crabbe [at the theatre]… [next day] I was particularly disappointed at seeing nothing of Mr Crabbe. I felt sure of him when I saw the boxes were fitted up with Crimson velvet.

(It doesn't sound as though Jane has met Crabbe in the company of Aunt Jane Leigh Perrot)

Letter from Mrs Leigh-Perrot to Mrs Austen (between 1815 and 1828)

...when I reflect on what might have been the consequences if the Stoneleigh settlement had not occasioned us such an increase of property as to enable us to bear up against our losses [occasioned by Henry's failure at his bank], I am thankful it is no worse. Where would my pretty Scarlets have gone then? I wish you thought as fondly of this place as I must ever do [the Austen's didn't like the house then?] – perhaps as it is the only house I have known for more than fifty years I may be partial to it as you may be to Steventon.

Extract from 'Emma' published in 1815

Mrs Goddard was the mistress of a School – not of a seminary, or an establishment, or anything which professed, in long sentences of refined nonsense, to combine liberal acquirements with elegant morality upon new principles and new systems – and where young ladies for enormous pay might be screwed out of health and into vanity.

(The sort of establishment where Jane Cholmeley {Mrs Leigh-Perrot} was educated?)

Letter 155 to Fanny Knight from Chawton 23–25 March 1817

... indeed. I shall be very glad when the Event [proving of her Uncle's Will] at Scarlets is over, the expectation of it keeps us in a worry, our Grandmama especially; she sits brooding over Evils which cannot be remedied & Conduct impossible to be understood.

Letter 157 to Charles Austen from Chawton 6 April 1817

My dearest Charles, Many thanks for your affectionate Letter … I have been suffering from a bilious attack, attended with a good deal of fever. A few days ago, my complaint appeared removed, but I am ashamed to say that the shock of my Uncle's Will brought on a relapse – I was so ill on Friday & thought myself so likely to be worse that I could not but press for Cassandra's returning with Frank after the Funeral last night, which she of course did … My aunt felt the value of Cassandra's company so fully, & was so very kind to her, & is poor Woman! so miserable at present (for her affliction has very much increased since the first) that we feel more regard for her than we ever did before.

Caroline Austen described her arrival at Scarlets in 1820

The coach put us down at the entrance to the lane and my brother and I walked up to the house and had to introduce ourselves to its mistress, whom I had never seen before, nor he since the early days of childhood…

(*Just a few months before he died, the Rev James Austen responded to a hint from his aunt that she wanted to see his children. He sent them to Scarlets, joining them after a visit to his doctor in London*)

Letter from Mrs George Austen to Mrs Leigh Perrot 4 January 1820

I sincerely thank you for your letter and its very kind contents; most thankfully do I accept your generous offer, such an addition to my income will be most acceptable at this time, and I will thank you if you will order Messrs Hoare every half year to place the money to my account...

(*This offer from Mrs Leigh Perrot was £100 per annum compensation for loss of income from Mrs Austen's son James who had died the previous month.*)

Letter from Mrs Leigh Perrot to Rev B Rudge, Bath. 3 July 1823

... I have let my pretty little Cottage on a lease from Midsummer Day – Mr Green at Wargrave (a most intelligent Friendly Man) recommends the Tennant; and indeed, has been very useful to each Party ...

Extract from one of the many poems written by J.E.A.L. when staying at Scarlets. October 1824

And thus, like the Sailor, but O! not for ever!
From this newly found region of bliss must we haste;
And stern stubborn distance must far from us sever
What is *near* in remembrance and *home* to our taste.

Letter from Mrs Leigh-Perrot 1828

Scarlets has been too much endeared to me from the association of domestic enjoyment, to be left to the management of one whose professional duties might call him out of the Kingdom, by which it might have been let or given up to children or improper manager.

(*Mrs Leigh-Perrot changed her mind about the inheritance of Scarlets when she preferred James Austen's choice of wife to that of his uncle Francis – Jane's brother*)

Letter from Emma, wife of J.E.A.L.
…Mrs Leigh Perrot is not at all a stupid person, she is a ladylike little old woman and though for years she has been quite out of the world, yet she once lived in it and talks very agreeably of past times.

Letter from Jane Leigh-Perrot referring to her husband. 1833
I can remember the applauding smile which gladden my Heart that said I was Valued and of consequence to one whose good opinion was everything to me.

A memory of Mary Augusta Austen Leigh upon moving into Scarlets
… Meanwhile those left at Scarlets worked hard in overlooking all its contents … the mahogany furniture, which went back to the days of Chippendale or Sheraton … was placed in the bedrooms, and the drawing room was before long renovated in the early Victorian style with a flowery carpet, gilt consoles, and pale green damask curtains … There were also a very large number of old framed prints on the walls … The Leigh Perrots must in their early married life have been great lovers of china. They had collected a large quantity of the blue-and-white, and a good deal of Worcester

and Chelsea china … The finest pair of vases, or figures …
remained to ornament the drawing room.

Sonning

Synopsis

In Jane Austen's day, Sonning would have been less busy than now and the main road probably more hazardous (although 21st-century potholes can be in keen competition). Nevertheless, it was an important Thames crossing place even then and the London to Bath stagecoach stopped at The Bull next to the church.

John Treacher built Sonning's fine brick bridge during <u>Dr Edward Cooper</u>'s residence, replacing the ancient wooden structures that had caused much controversy. (Two small bridges were replaced in 1905)

Treacher's bridge. The tower of St. Andrews can be seen amongst the trees on the right.

St. Andrew's church underwent many alterations and additions during the Victorian age.

The board which hangs on one of the pillars inside the church, lists Edward Cooper on the right-hand column, halfway down

The river would have been busy with barges rather than pleasure craft as it was very much a highway for transporting goods in those days; but the walk along its banks at Sonning was and still is, a pleasant exercise.

Many churches have undergone considerable alterations and additions during the Victorian age and St Andrew's is no exception. In common with other churches, there is a board listing the vicars of the church. This one tells us that Dr

Edward Cooper, Jane Austen's uncle, was vicar from 1784 until 1792.

We have already seen that the Austen's connection with Sonning is through the Cooper family. Dr Edward Cooper, who probably knew the village as 'Sunning', was the son of Gislington Cooper who, during the time when the Leighs were living in the area, was residing with his family at Phyllis Court, a resplendent country house on the banks of the River Thames at Henley. Edward Cooper married Cassandra's sister Jane Leigh. They were first at Southcote, which is on the west of Reading with Sonning on the east, both on the Bath Road. The young Edward Cooper (Jane Austen's cousin) was born at Southcote as was his sister Jane and it was soon after the daughter's birth that the Coopers moved to Bath.

However, after Mrs Cooper's tragic death, Dr Cooper retreated to the familiar comfort of the Thames Valley and became resident vicar of Sonning in July 1784.

Boxed pews had been in short supply in the church and in 1783 William Martin built a gallery in the north aisle. All went smoothly until in 1791, one of the 'owners' accepted as a pew-tenant, was a newcomer to the village who refused to pay up and complained to the Dean on his next visitation. The Rev Edward Cooper was instructed to interrogate every member of his congregation to ascertain the general feeling about private galleries. The gallery was then firmly restricted to the owners' families, guests, servants and tenants; and so it continued for sixty years. As the vicar, Dr Cooper, in 1785, had other duties one of which was to sign the rate for the necessary relief of the poor of Sonning. Signing documents and registers would have been a less arduous task for a very sick man, than quizzing his parishioners.

Mrs Philip Lybbe Powys often mentions the Coopers in her diaries. They knew each other socially – Jane Cooper and the young Caroline Powys were friends – and probably because of this, it resulted in the union between Dr Cooper's son Edward Cooper and the daughter Caroline Isobel Powys whose connection with the area has been acknowledged in the Harpsden pages. We have no record of the younger Edward Cooper residing in Sonning but he must have done so when not actually at Eton or at university in Oxford. When he married Caroline Powys, they went to live at Harpsden, Edward taking up the appointment as Curate there.

Jane Leigh, as we have seen, married Edward Cooper in 1768. Whilst they were living in Bath, her daughter Jane was educated with the Austen sisters in Oxford by Mrs Cawley, her sister-in-law. Mrs Cawley took the children to Southampton where they contracted 'a putrid fever' – presumably typhus. Mrs Austen and Mrs Cooper went to Southampton to rescue the girls. Unfortunately, Mrs Cooper caught the fever and died. As a remembrance of Aunt Jane, Dr Cooper sent a ring 'representing a sprig of diamonds, with one emerald' to Cassandra, and to Jane he sent a headband which on several occasions she proudly wore at balls. Mrs Cooper was never a resident of Sonning. After the death of her mother and the removal to Sonning of her father, Jane Cooper was sent, with the Austen girls, to the Abbey School in Reading. At the end of her education there, she lived on and off with her father at Sonning but spent most of her time at Steventon with the Austens until she married from there in 1792.

The Lybbe-Powys diaries are the source which gives us an insight into Dr Cooper's last days. Although described as a 'rosy round-faced divine, with a most amiable expression', by 1792 he was a sick man, and a holiday in company with his daughter Jane, Mrs Powys and her daughter Caroline to the Lake District, had to be cancelled so they went to the Isle of Wight instead. (Do I detect shades of *Pride and Prejudice* here?) After their return on 8 August, the Powys went to dinner at Sonning and stayed the night. Mrs Powys was not happy with the Doctor's health, although she felt that the time on the Isle of Wight had done him some good. However, three weeks later, Dr Edward Cooper died and was buried at Whaddon, Bath, with his wife.

Supporting evidence

The Diary of Mrs Philip Lybbe Powys 2 June 1790
Dr and Miss Cooper came to fetch Caroline, to go with them to the review on the following day. The first time I had ever parted for a night with my dear girl, tho then fifteen.

The Diary of Mrs Philip Lybbe Powys 21 July 1792
Mr Powys, Caroline, and myself, went to Dr Cooper's at Sonning, and set off the next morning on our tour to the isle of Wight.

The Diary of Mrs Philip Lybbe Powys, 8 Aug 1792 on their return from the Isle of Wight
Wheatsheaf Inn. The next morning, the family of the Austens breakfasted with us [here].

(*The Wheatsheaf Inn was in Popham. Here the Austen's*

collected their post whilst living in Steventon and it was a staging post for them and their visitors.)

The Diary of Mrs Philip Lybbe Powys August 1792

…and got about five to dinner at Dr Cooper's at Sonning; lay there that night, and got home to Fawley to dinner on August 9 after a most pleasant tour, which we should all have enjoyed in a much greater degree had we not visibly seen poor Dr Cooper's health daily declining, though the journey seemed to have been of service as often as we changed the air; but at last we thought him too far gone to be at any great distance from home, and entreated him to return, which he always seemed unwilling to do, perhaps thinking it might be less anxiety to his children if he had died at any other place, as never were father and children more fond or attentive to each other's happiness.

August 27 Died at his living at Sonning, the Rev Dr Cooper very much regretted by all his friends.

The Diary of Mrs Philip Lybbe Powys August 1798

We, that morning received a letter from our son Thomas, with the most melancholy intelligence of the death of Lady Williams [Jane Cooper] by a most unfortunate accident. As she was driving herself in a whisky, a dray-horse ran away and drove against the chaise, by which she was thrown out and killed on the spot. Never spoke after. We were so alarmed for our dear Mr Cooper whose health had been so bad for some time, and who was one of the most affectionate of brothers, that we were quite miserable, and wrote immediately to Caroline…

Letter 24 to Cassandra from Steventon 1 November 1800

I wore at the Ball your favourite gown, a bit of muslin of the same round my head, bordered with Mrs Cooper's band and one little comb.

Shiplake

Synopsis

On the Oxfordshire side of the river, between Sonning and Henley, is where Emily Climenson, wife of the vicar of Shiplake and the editor of *The Diaries of Mrs Philip Lybbe Powys*, lived at the end of the nineteenth century.

Some decades earlier, Alfred Lord Tennyson was married there. This was the poet who, when he saw Lyme and his friends, spoke of the reputed landing place of the Duke of Monmouth, became indignant as he would rather see the Cobb. He was, of course, referring to the famous incident in *Persuasion*. Tennyson rated Jane Austen's work next to that of Shakespeare.

Supporting evidence

From Persuasion Chapter XII

… he put out his hands; she was too precipitate by half a second, she fell on the pavement on the Lower Cobb, and was taken up lifeless!

Comments from Alfred Lord Tennyson

"Don't talk to me of the Duke of Monmouth. Show me the exact spot where Louisa Musgrove fell."

From 'Marriage Morning' by Alfred Lord Tennyson

Vicar of this pleasant spot
Where it was my chance to marry
Happy, happy be your lot
In the vicarage by the quarry.

Dedication in Passages from the Diaries of Mrs Philip Lybbe Powys of Hardwick House, Oxon 1756–1808 by Emily J Climenson

To
My dear friends, the Elder Branch of the
Lybbe Powys, of Hardwick,
I dedicate this effort of pleasing toil in collating
And noting, the interesting Diaries of their
Clever and charming ancestress
EMILY J CLIMENSON
Shiplake Vicarage, March 1899

Reading

Synopsis

Reading stands above Caversham, the River Thames separating them, in the triangle where the Kennet flows into the Thames. Long before <u>Jane Austen</u> went to school in Reading, the <u>Leighs</u>, the <u>Coopers</u>, the <u>Powys</u> and the <u>Austens</u> knew the town. Reading is Berkshire's county town and had a large, popular market. It was close enough to Harpsden, Hardwick, Sonning and Scarlets to be a centre for shopping, entertainment, reviews, races and social intercourse for the people who concern us. There were thriving pin-making and silk-weaving industries in the town, making it a good place to buy ribbons, scarves and material. It was also a major stopping place for anyone travelling.

The Bear Inn, Reading.

Mary Lascelles says that 'the first recorded happening is [Jane Austen's] visit, with Cassandra, in 1782, to a connection of their mother's followed shortly by a stay of a year or two at a school in Reading'. As Dr Cooper did not move to Sonning until 1784 and had moved from Southcote to Bath when his daughter Jane was born in 1772, who could it have been? The Leigh-Perrots at Scarlets? The Powys at Hardwick Hall?

Who knows what discussion took place in the Austen household or between Jane's parents and Uncle Cooper after the schooling by Mrs Cawley had so spectacularly failed? Did Mrs Austen's relations recommend the Abbey School having heard good reports for the Reading area? After his wife's fatal experience in Southampton and the subsequent move of Dr Edward Cooper to Sonning, did he decide upon the school in Reading for his daughter and suggest that Jane and <u>Cassandra Austen</u> should go too when it still retained a good reputation?

Was Jane Cooper already a scholar there before the Austen girls joined her?

The Abbey School – Print from Reading Library

Besides other amenities of the town for shopping, eating, visiting the theatre, attending assemblies and concerts or an itinerary stop, there was an education for boys at the reputable Reading Boys School under the headship of the well-known Dr Valpy. A street where the school once stood is named after Dr Valpy. A rough open space used as their playground was next to the remains of the inner gateway of the abbey (partly now accessing Forbury Gardens). This was where a respectable counterpart for young ladies was housed, run by Mrs La Tournelle. George Holbert Tucker tells us that 'Earlier biographers of Jane Austen have maintained that her regular schooling ended in 1784 when she was nine, but later research indicates the sisters presumably remained at the Abbey School until 1786'. This seems to be on the strength of payments made by George Austen through his bank, but the exact date is still up for debate.

Another gateway was designed by Gilbert Scott and built in 1861 because the ancient abbey gateway had collapsed. Fox-Talbot photographed the original building in 1845 before it crumbled. His view through the gateway looks north and shows open fields crossed paths leading to the Thames and woods at Caversham. Alas, the railways changed all this. After Mr Brunel's line from Paddington cut through the area between it and the abbey and Caversham Bridge the two areas were gradually filled in by houses and industrial or commercial units. Today, if you stand where the gateway once stood, your view will be curtailed by very tall commercial buildings. You cannot even see the railway and the busy and fast IDR comes between the buildings and Forbury Gardens.

Two vast stairways with the remains of gilt on the balustrades led to the room above the gateway. These were connected by narrow passages full of nooks and crannies, to the adjoining schoolhouse – a rambling two-storey building shaded by huge trees under which the younger children played on summer evenings.

The Stranger in Reading, (John Man) writing, some twenty-five years later but very little different, in 1810 when the Abbey School for Girls was no longer situated there, tells us that 'the Forbury, on the south and west sides, was enclosed with houses, a part of the church-yard, and the magnificent ruins of the abbey … and on the north, was a long terrace walk, bounded by a low wall, affording a delightful view of the Oxfordshire hills, clothed with woods, interspersed with rich corn fields, and gentlemen's seats, extending one beyond the other as far as the eye can reach'. One of these 'seats' at Caversham, was where Charles I was held just before his beheading, and perhaps Jane had him in her thoughts when she looked out in that direction. Viewing Reading through rose-tinted glasses a year earlier, William Fordyce Mavor, vicar of Hurley, praised Reading for its air of gentility and Mary Russell Mitford, writing at the end of the eighteenth century would agree with him. Fairs were held in Forbury and if at school, the girls would have been able to look down upon them from above the gateway. At Candlemas, the fair was for selling horses and two occasions later (May Day and St James Feast Day – 25 July) the fair would be for selling cows and horses. Perhaps the one In September would have been of less interest as it was a Hiring Day. Cheeses were sold at Fairs and the one at Reading was the best in the country at the time. One wonders if some found their way to Steventon.

The Abbey has a venerable past. A monk is credited with composing in the 13th century, the endless canon 'Summer is icumen in': the earliest example of secular music. Did Miss Pitts teach the boarders to sing this song? The melancholy Henry I is buried here (the fruitless subject of a recent archaeological dig). The Abbey was dissolved by Henry VIII and the Civil War did not pass it by. The discovery of a skeleton and the number of macabre stories of death circulating in the school are more than sufficient to conjure up spectres in the ancient ruins – a suitable background for a Gothic tale or two and the building sufficiently awesome to remind <u>Caroline Powys</u> of Mrs Radcliffe. It was probably out of bounds to the girls. The stories of Reading Abbey's glorious and not-so-glorious past must surely have had some bearing on Jane's attitude and knowledge when she wrote *The History of England* and even *Northanger Abbey*.

Provided the girls appeared in the tutor's study for a few hours each morning, they could spend the rest of the day gossiping in the turrets (from Mrs Sherwood's recollections), die of laughing, lounge in the garden, read recommended or smuggled books or look out of the window above the gateway, quite undisturbed by Mrs La Tournelle. At the same time, the domestic arrangements were admirably clean and comfortable. St Lawrence Church is hard by and no doubt the girls were crocodile-walked there for a Sunday service (where they might come into visual contact with Dr Valpy's boys) if they hadn't been taken out to attend their own local Church – for instance to Sonning. Mrs La Tournelle may have led the girls to church on her wooden leg (not a cork leg – Cork Street was where wooden legs were made) or more likely by Miss Pitt. Besides eye contact in church, there was an opportunity for closer fraternising as the girls were joined by the Valpy boys in dances and theatrical productions in a large hall at the Abbey school.

Much of what we know about Jane Austen's days at the Abbey School comes from the recollections of Mrs Sherwood who was at that same school but several years later. Unfortunately, we are given a rather downbeat picture of Mrs Sarah La Tournelle – Mrs Hackett. However, thanks to Mark Burgess and his article in the JAS Report for 2018, we can revise our view of this lady. She comes, in fact, from a respectable, educated family, her father a rector named George Bell. Like Jane Austen, Mrs La Tournelle's father died reducing the family of three girls to hardship. Unlike Emma's sister in *The Watsons*, they opted for a life as teachers. At this moment in time, Mrs La Tournelle's name was Esther Bell. She married Peter Hackett in 1747 but nine years later hit on hard times. Esher Hackett found herself teaching in Reading, her husband and a young daughter still residing in London. She lost her husband in 1767 and her daughter married in 1773. Esther Hackett was now responsible for herself. Perhaps she found her surname rather unfortunate as a teacher, but thinking perhaps that a French name would be more alluring than Bell, she became Mrs Sarah (a form of Esther) La Tournelle and was soon proprietress of the Abbey School where she was highly successful. Mrs Sherwood knew her only in her last years when she was quite happy for her assistants to take on much of the responsibilities and work of teaching. A real French teacher was working at the school and married Miss Pitts who had been there for some years.

I for one, having read this article, have certainly revised my opinion of Mrs La Tournelle and think that Jane's education was probably rather better than Mrs Sherwood's. Perhaps when Jane described Mrs Goddard's school as 'where girls may be sent to be out of the way' it was an acerbic tongue or perhaps she was roasting her parents who had sent her to Reading under those circumstances. And maybe Jane was remembering the Abbey School teachers when she was writing *The Watsons*.

The school went bankrupt in 1794 after Mrs La Tournelle had moved on, running and/or taking up teaching in other establishments, ending up in Henley where she died and was buried.

Reading was an easy town to reach and handy for friends and relations to visit or be visited. We do not know if the Leigh-Perrots from Scarlets, Dr Cooper from Sonning or Caroline Powys now moved to Fawley, ever took the girls out to tea or to shop in Reading. We do know, however, that one October, <u>Thomas Leigh</u> (Jane's mother's cousin) called in on his way home from London to Adlestrop and gave Cassandra and Jane exactly half a guinea apiece. What would they spend it on? What opportunity would they have to spend it? On another occasion, far more exciting, their glamourous brother <u>Edward</u> came with his cousin <u>Edward Cooper</u> and took all three girls out to dine at an inn (perhaps The Crown in Crown Street or the Bear in Bridge Street) There may have been tea rooms where patisseries were sold. One can only speculate who conveyed the girls between Reading and Steventon.

In March 2006, the Jane Austen Society made possible the mounting of a commemorative plaque by the side of the present gateway.

JANE AUSTEN
Novelist
Attended school at the Abbey Gateway
1785-6
Plaque unveiled by H.H. Judge Spence
Resident Judge, Reading Crown Court
24 July 2006

Jane and Cassandra left the Abbey School in 1785/6 but, as witnessed in her letter of 1813, it was not the last time she was in Reading. As is the case nowadays, the town was a major crossroads for the busy Bath Road (now the A4) and Oxford Road (A329) – rather unnervingly called Cemetery Junction. Another important road (A33) connects Reading with Basingstoke and Southampton or the southwestern counties of Devon and Cornwall. Jane knew the town as a staging post: The Bear, (or Black Bear where Mrs Lybbe Powys regularly stayed when setting out on her travels) a principal coaching inn, was on the Bath Road down from Castle Hill in the west. Silas Tomkyn Camberbache alias Samuel Taylor Coleridge stayed here in 1794. He praised Jane Austen's 'truth and individuality'. The Crown, also on the Bath Road, was east of the town at the top of London Street where the main road sets out from Reading to Southampton via Basingstoke.

According to Rupert Willoughby, there is a remarkable serendipity which connects Reading, Oxford and Tonbridge. Thomas White was born in Reading in 1492 and married Mary Kibblewhite of South Fawley (now there's another coincidence). He was Sheriff of London in 1547 and Mayor of London in 1553. He was knighted in the same year by Queen Mary I and a member of the commission for the trial of Lady Jane Grey (more facts that would have interested Jane). White became very rich and poured some of his wealth into the foundation of St John's College in Oxford.

In a Charter of 1554, of the fifty places, one was for a boy at Tonbridge School – founded by a close friend of Thomas White. In 1774, George Austen was the fortunate pupil of Tonbridge School who was awarded the White Scholarship. (Other Austen boys attending St John's college, benefited through 'Founder's kin') One source says that a pupil of George Austen's in 1786 was the son of Henry Deane, Mayor of Reading. The young (George?) Deane was admitted to St John's College, Oxford – an amazing co-incidence – as White's scholar, being Founder's Kin.

Reading was well-known to the Austens long after Jane died. It continued to be a major staging post and when Brunel built his Great Western Railway, Reading Station was opened in March 1840. The same year in which the railway came to Reading it also came through the Chawton area, with Alton being the nearest station. As late as 1848, just before her death, Jane's sister Cassandra was in Reading.

Jane Austen's connections continued to occur in Reading through the Victorian era. (Lefroy nieces lived here) Next door to the ruins of the Abbey is Reading Gaol where Oscar Wilde was infamously detained at Her Majesty's pleasure. Whilst he was an inmate, besides writing his well-known *Ballad*, he thought that there should be a better stock of books in the library and composed a list of preferred authors, including Jane Austen. Did he know that he was living next door to her school? (Toad of Toad Hall was also imprisoned there but I cannot find any Austen connection to him.) There are those who would like to see the now disbanded prison turned into an Arts Centre – or even devoted to Jane Austen and other literary notables of the town, such as Mary Russell Mitford, even Samuel Taylor Coleridge, Toad of Toad Hall. The late Deidre Le Faye, the best authority on all things Austen, attended the present Abbey School (now in Kendrick Road) that claims affinity with that attended by Jane Austen. It is certainly a tenuous one, the original having re-located in Reading after a sojourn in London, practically next door to one of Henry's residents, and whilst there visited by Jane. The school also had a brief sojourn in France (I think Paris).

Reading academics continue to discover connections and write articles and books with Jane Austen as the central figure or as a catalyst.

Supporting evidence

The Diary of Mrs Lybbe Powys 1760
We that evening reached Reading, the county town of Berks. Is large, well-built, and during the Civil War in England was strongly fortified. The remains of the bastions &c are still seen; formerly was noted for a famous abbey in the adjoining Fourbourg [Forbury]

Mr Austen's Bank Account 1785–7

S La Tournelle
Aug 20th 1785£37 – 19 – 0
Feb 13th 1786£36 – 2 – 6
Jan 2nd 1787£16 – 0 – 0

The Diary of Mrs Lybbe Powys August 1788
The races not good, the balls tolerably full, considering how many families at this season leave their seats in the country for the different watering-places now in vogue.

Itinerary: July 7 Monday Breakfasted at Maidenhead at Orkney Arms

Lay at Reading, Black Bear

July 8 Tuesday, went to Beenham and returned to Reading

Reading Mercury 6 April 1789

This day was published, price 3d
(To be continued weekly)
No IX of
The LOITERER
Printed for the author and sold by C S Rann Oxford; Mess. Edgertons, Whitehall, London; Mess. Pearson and Rollason, Birmingham; Mr Maylor, Bath; and Mess. Smart and Cowslade, Reading.

Of whom may be had any of the former numbers.

[*It could be that the Austen subscribed to the Reading Mercury regularly. From her letters, we know that Jane had access to this newspaper from time to time. This edition seems to be the only one where The Loiterer is advertised. Could it be because of the inclusion of a letter from Sophia Sentiment?*]

Mary Russell Mitford writing in the 1790s

… [Reading is]clean, airy and affluent; well paved, well lighted; well watched; abounding in wide and spacious streets filled with excellent shops and handsome houses.

Letter 4 to Cassandra from Rowling, Kent 1 Sept 1796

My Dearest Cassandra,

The letter which I have this moment received from you has diverted me beyond moderation. I could die of laughter at it, as they used to say at school.

Extract from 'The Watsons', Jane Austen's unfinished novel presumably written in Bath

"I could rather do anything than be teacher at a school," said her [Emma's] sister. "I have been at school, Emma, and know what life they lead; *you* never have."

(Was Jane Austen remembering a lot of the teachers at the Abbey school?)

1809 William Fordyce Mavor 'General View of the Agriculture of Berkshire'.

The houses [in Reading] are chiefly built of brick, well-built and commodious; and the streets are spaciously and handsomely paved. An air of gentility is thrown over the place, and there is an elegant sociability in the manners of the inhabitants, which is irresistibly attractive to strangers

1810 – Jon Man (the Stranger in Reading)

… this is a poor industrious fellow who traverses the streets from morning 'til night, with a large basket on each arm, filled with cakes and other rarities for children; continually calling out 'Nice new! Nice new!' 'Here they be!' 'Two sized bigger than last week!'

Extract from 'Sense and Sensibility' published in 1811

Their party was small and the hours passed quietly away. Mrs Palmer had her child, and Mrs Jennings her carpet-work; they talked of the friends they had left behind, arranged Lady Middleton's engagements and wondered whether Mr Palmer and Colonel Brandon would get farther than Reading that night.

Letter 85 to Cassandra from Sloane Street 20 May 1813

… I should not wonder if we got no father than Reading on Thursday evening and so reach Steventon only to a reasonable Dinner hour the next day.

Extract from 'Emma' published in 1815

Mrs Goddard was the mistress of a School…a real, honest, old-fashioned Boarding-school, where a reasonable quantity of accomplishments were sold at a reasonable price, and where girls might be sent to be out of the way and scramble themselves into a little education, without any danger of coming back prodigies.

(*It is thought that this paragraph is reminiscent of Jane Austen's time at Reading Abbey School*)

The journal of Charles Knight (Jane Austen's nephew) winter 1845

... called on At Cassra [Aunt Cassandra] and took leave of Cassra Austen, who was to go next day with my A[un]t to Reading on her way home [to Cornwall]

Anna Lefroy's [Jane's niece] Original Memories of Jane Austen (quoted in J.E.A.L.'s 'Memoir')

My Grandmother [Mrs Austen] talking to me once [of] bygone times & of that particular time when my Aunts were placed at the Reading Abbey School said that Jane was too young to make her going to school at all necessary, but it was her own doing, she would go with Cassandra; "if Cassandra's head had been going to be cut off, Jane would have her's [sic] cut off too."

Mapledurham, Purley
and Whitchurch

Synopsis

Mapledurham in Oxfordshire, with Whitchurch further upriver, are on one side of the Thames and Purley opposite on the Berkshire side of the river. Jane Austen's association with these three Thameside villages is tenuous, to say the least, but she almost certainly knew of them, if she didn't pass them by on her travels.

As a reader, familiar with the works of Alexander Pope, Jane would have known that he was an admirer of the two young Blount ladies who lived at Mapledurham House downriver from Hardwick House and was a frequent visitor there. As Cassandra Leigh (Mrs George Austen) and Caroline Girle (Mrs Philip Powys) were only five and six years old at the time of Pope's death, they are highly unlikely to have known him although they almost certainly knew of him and the connection with Mapledurham. Caroline Powys visited the Blounts and the Leighs may have done so, too.

There was a closer link to Pope, however, through George Austen whose father was educated at Sevenoaks Grammar School where his tutor was Elijah Fenton. After leaving the school, Fenton became an assistant to Pope and helped him with his translation of *The Odyssey.*

The Gates of Purley Hall

With one's back to Purley Hall on the Berkshire bank, if the twenty-first century did not intrude in the form of hedges and the railway, it would be possible to see Hardwick house on the opposite bank of the Thames. Warren Hastings, of whose connection Jane Austen fans will be well aware, rented Purley Hall and lived there whilst awaiting his trial, moving to Windsor when it began in 1788. It is known that Henry visited Hastings regularly at his Gloucestershire home at Daylesford and occasionally at Windsor when Hastings lived there during his trial. It is not impossible that Henry called in to visit Hastings when he lodged at Purley Hall on his way to or from Oxford. It was the years when Jane Austen was at school in Reading. Henry matriculated at Oxford in 1788 but Hastings may have moved away from Purley Hall by that time. For the Austens to travel between Steventon and Oxford, there were two options once they had reached Reading. (Unless they went via Newbury) One was to go via

Henley (and we have seen that Henry did that at least once when he called in at Harpsden) and the other is to travel on the Oxford Road going via Streatley, the two roads meeting at Wallingford. Perhaps Cassandra and Jane were taken this way when they went to school, although they may have met up with Jane Cooper in Bath and travelled to Oxford from that town.

The River Thames flows wide and straight, the countryside open and pleasant, between Purley and Basildon with the Oxford Road (A329) as its close companion. Before Basildon, it reaches the twin villages of Pangbourne on the Berkshire bank and Whitchurch on the other side of the river, reached by a ferry until 1793, but now bridged where one still pays a toll to cross – too late for <u>Cassandra Leigh</u> who many, many times visited her friends <u>Thomas</u> and <u>Philip Powys</u> at Hardwick House in Whitchurch, to walk across to Pangbourne. A ford existed, however, and the young people may have enjoyed splashing through it on one of their rides. Cassandra Leigh's friend <u>Caroline Girle</u> married Philip Lybbe Powys in 1762 so the visits to Hardwick Hall will probably have become more frequent during the two years before the Leighs left Harpsden for Bath.

Hardwick Hall from the Thames path

Today it is possible to walk the 3½ miles from Pangbourne to Mapledurham, thanks to the Thames Path, on the Berkshire side of the river. Halfway along, there is a splendid view of both the stables and Hardwick House itself.

After she had moved to Steventon, there may not have been times when Mrs Austen travelled from Hampshire to Oxford via Reading and the Oxford road, certainly not with her daughters. However, if James or Henry were going that way she would certainly have told them to look out for landmarks of Purley Hall gates and the view across the Thames to Hardwick House, no doubt regaling them with reminiscences and giving them a history lesson of the Civil War at the same time and the glorious part played in those events by the Leighs of Stoneleigh Abbey, the Lybbes of Hardwick House and the Midlands and the Blounts of Mapledurham.

The dark red Tudor brickwork of Hardwick, its gables and clustering chimneys were accompanied by elms that perhaps

Charles I saw as saplings when he amused himself playing bowls on the Lybbe manor when he was held captive at Caversham Park. It was at an inn at Colly's End on 19 July 1648, when he came to bowl on the green above the house, attended by a troop of Colonel Rossiter's horse.

The diaries of Caroline Lybbe Powys include a comprehensive description of her visit to Derbyshire and meeting the Devonshire of Chatsworth House. Was Jane Austen the recipient of her reminiscences at any time? If so, was it whilst she was at school in Reading and taken out to tea by her mother's old friend? Or did Caroline Powys visit the Austen's at Steventon? She certainly halted at Popham in the company of the Coopers when they went to the Isle of Wight and met them for breakfast on the way home. There are some who think that Jane Austen had this background knowledge when she was writing *Pride and Prejudice* soon after that journey to the Hampshire island. It could have come second-hand from Mrs Austen, of course.

Elizabeth I visited Hardwick House and the Lybbes were fined for their support of the Stuart cause. I cannot believe that Cassandra (Leigh) Austen did not relate these romantic stories of Tudor and Stuart times, both of here and Stoneleigh Abbey (where Charles I had been sheltered and they had been prepared to shelter Prince Charles Edward) to her children in Jane's formative years. Yes, the Lybbe, Powys and Leigh families had a lot in common.

Supporting evidence

*Poetic lines on a wooden board affixed to Hardwick House
after Charles I played bowls on their manor*
    Stop, traveller – stop: within this peaceful shade
    His favourite game the Royal Martyr play'd;
    Deprived of honours, fortune, friends and rank,
    Drank from the bowl, and bowl'd for what he drank;
    Sought in a cheerful glass his cares to drown
    And chang'd a guinea, ere he lost a crown

*(There is no date attached to this poem. It may have been
composed by Tom Powys around the time of another of his in 1756.
It is in his style)*

Extract from a poem by Alexander Pope 1714
    Epistle to Miss Blount on her Leaving Town after the
Coronation
    As some fond virgin, whom her mother's care
    Drags from the town to wholesome country air,
    Just when she learns to roll a melting eye,
    And her spark, yet think no danger nigh;
    She went, to plain work, and to purling brooks
    Old-fashioned halls, dull aunts, and croaking rooks
    She went from Op'ra, park, assembly, play
    To morning walks, and prayers three hours a day;
    To pass her time, twixt reading and bohea,
    To muse, and spill her solitary tea…

*(Pope went courting the two Miss Blounts and it is thought that
he often rowed himself along the river to Mapledurham. (From*

Sonning or Reading, which would be the nearest points from where he lived in Binfield.) He also wrote Epistle to Miss Blount in 1710. Pope went to live in Binfield between Wokingham and Easthampstead. It was whilst living there that he introduced Elijah Fenton {from Tonbridge School} to the owner of Easthampstead Park as a tutor to his son.)

Memorial to Elijah Fenton, who died in July 1730, in Easthampstead church (this village is also in the Thames Valley and, like Sonning, part of Wokingham district) includes this epitaph by Alexander Pope.

This modest stone what few vain marbles can
May truly say, here lies an honest man
A poet blest beyond the poets fate
Whom heav'n left sacred from the proud and great
Foe to loud praise and friend to learned ease
Content with science in the vale of peace
Calmly he look'd on either life & here
Saw nothing to regret, or there to fear
From natur's temp'rate feast rose satisfied
Thanked heav'n that he had lived and that he died.

Lines by Tom Powys in 1756, were painted onto a wooden plaque and erected above the name of Straw Hall on the Hardwick estate.

Within this cot no polished marble shines
Nor the rich product of Arcadian mines;
The glare of splendour and the toys of state
Resigned, unenvied, to the proud and great;
Whilst here reclining, these noble scenes you view
Which Nature's bold, unguided pencil drew

The Diary of Mrs Phillip Lybbe Powys 1757

…She took us to see a house of the Duke of Devonshire's…We tried one evening to ascend the prodigious rock I before spoke of, called Matlock High Tor. Many do, it seems, perform it, but I own I was frightened before I had got a quarter of the way up…

The Diary of Mrs Philip Lybbe Powys 5 August 1762

I was married to Philip Lybbe Powys of Hardwick Hall, [sic] Oxfordshire *and 24 October*. We live at Hardwick in a large old house, about twelve rooms on a floor, with four staircases, the situation delightful, on the declivity of a hill, the most beautiful woods behind, and a fine view of the Thames and rich meadows in front.

The Diary of Mrs Philip Lybbe Powys 1771

…We were talking of the amazing wit of Pope, who was often at Mawley, tho' much oftener at our neighbours the Blounts of Maple-Durham, where there are such fine portraits of himself and Patty Blount. One day, Sir Walter's father was in his company and talking of punning, Pope said that was a species of wit so triflingly easy that he would answer to make one on any proposed subject offhand, when a lady in the company said, "Well, Mr Pope, make one on keelhauling." He instantly replied, "That madam, is indeed putting a man under *hardship*!"

Letter 53 to Cassandra from Godmersham 20–22 June 1808

… dine with the Dean [Thomas Powys] who is just come to Canterbury.

Letter 87 to Cassandra from Henrietta Street 15–16 September 1813

... and Mr Hastings – I am quite delighted with what such a man writes about it [*Pride and Prejudice*] Henry sent him the Books after his return from Daylesford – but you will hear the Letter too. ... ... Nothing has been done as to *S & S*. The Books came to hand too late for him to have time for it, before he went. Mr Hastings never hinted at Eliza in the smallest degree.

(Henry married his cousin Eliza de Feuillide in 1797. She was the goddaughter and beneficiary of Warren Hastings {some think his daughter} and had died just before Henry's visit referred to in this letter.)

Basildon

Synopsis

Eric de Mare writes that 'The architects of the time [Georgian] went in frankly for show rather than use of domestic convenience and brought from [Alexander] Pope his well-known protest:

'Tis very fine,

But where d'ye sleep, or where d'ye dine?

I see from all you have been telling

That tis a house, but not a dwelling.'

As a reader of Pope, it is a sentiment that would amuse Jane. The National Trust guide to Basildon Park informs us, 'The fact that Clive tried to buy it in 1767, before settling on Claremont, and that Randolph Marriott was one of his and Francis Sykes eventual purchase in 1771, the present house being built by him between 1776 and 1783.' Francis Sykes was a close friend of Warren Hastings [explaining Hastings' temporary renting of Purley Hall] and it was he who had brought Hastings' son to England to hand over to George and Cassandra Austen. Sadly, by the time Basildon House had been purchased and Warren Hastings returned to England, the young boy had died. In fact, the child died in the care of the Austens at Steventon.

More recently, our interest in Basildon Park arises from the fact that it became Netherfield in a production of *Pride and Prejudice*. Nick Shave, writing in *Classicfm Magazine*, describes the film, '…based on Jane Austen's turn of the 19th-century romance, it stars Donald Sutherland as the father of five girls who are eagerly elbowed into marriage by their mother (Brenda Blethyn). Keira Knightly plays the outspoken daughter, Elizabeth Bennet, who yearns her way through a confused yet romantic courtship with taciturn Mr Darcy (Matthew McFadden) then brings her face to face with the autocratic Lady Catherine de Bourgh (Judi Dench).'

In July 2017, to recognise the 200th anniversary of Jane Austen's death, BBC2 broadcast a programme entitled *My Friend Jane*. In this, Basildon Park has a five-minute share of fame when the picnic scene (in full Regency costume) was filmed on Basildon Park's own front lawn, the building a splendid backdrop, depicting what some years earlier was portrayed as Netherfield. Jane would have loved it.

Basildon Park and the lawn where the picnic was held in 2017

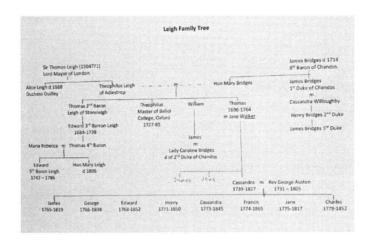

Leigh Family Tree

Sources:

Austen, Jane. *The History of England*
The Watsons
Sense and Sensibility
Pride and Prejudice
Mansfield Park
Emma
Persuasion
Northanger Abbey
Austen Leigh, J.E. *A Memoir of Jane Austen*
Baldwin, Jan. *Henley Heritage*
Camp, John. *A Portrait of Buckinghamshire*
Cawthorn, Martin J. *The Curious Case of the Schoolboy Who was Killed*
Classicfm. *Music at the Movies* Nick Shave
Climenson, Emily J ed. *The Diaries of Mrs Philip Lybbe Powys*
de Mare, Eric. *Time on the Thames*

Doody, Margaret. *Jane Austen's Names*

Elliott, Kirsten. *Anybody's favourite Aunt?*

Jane Austen's Regency World

JAS Report 1998. *Jane Austen and her brother Henry's bank failure*

T.A.B. Corley. *Mrs Sherwood's Secrets*

Chris Viveash. *Jane Austen and Maria Edgeworth*

Irene Collins (2001). *Too much zeal for the Bible Society*

Farnell Parsons (2002). *Jane Austen's Passage to Derbyshire*

Elizabeth Boardman (2003). *Mrs Cawley and Brasenose College,*

Carol Harley (2004). *It's to have a Crest*

Jane Hurst (2006). *The Jane Austen Dinner*

David Selwyn. *One of my Greatest Comforts*

Deirdre le Faye (2009). *Austen Papers 1704–1856: an updating*

Jane Hurst (2010). *Aunt Cassandra – a very great loss to us all*

Mark Burgess (2019). *Mrs La Tournelle, Jane Austen's Schoolmistress*

Le Faye, Deidre. *A Chronology of Jane Austen and Her Family*

Jane Austen's Letters Third Edition

Mann. *The Stranger in Reading*

Mindell, Ruth, and Johnathan. *Bridges over the Thames*

Perkins, Angela. *The Book of Sonning*

Phillips, Daphne. *The Great Road to Bath*

Roberts, Cecil. *And so to Bath*

Senior, W. *The Royal River*

Selwyn, David. Collected Poems of the Austen Family

Fugitive Pieces – The Poems of J. E. Austen Leigh

Slatter, Rev John. *The History of the Parish of Whitchurch* (Reading Library reserve collection)

Tyack, C. *Harpsden Church Parish Guide*

Uglow, Jenny. *The Lunar Men*

Wargrave Local History Society – *The Book of Wargrave*

Watkins, Susan. *Jane Austen's Town and Country Style*

Watson, Vera. *Mary Russell Mitford*

Whitehead, David C. *Henley on Thames a History*

Willoughby, Rupert. *Reading and its Contribution to World Literature*

…and biographies and studies by Bush, Butler, Byrne, Cecil, Chapman, Clery, Collins, Harman, Honan, Jenkins, Jenkyns, Lane, Lascelles, Le Faye, Mitton, Nicolson, Noakes, Pinion, Southam Spence, Tanner, Tomalin, Tucker et al. not specifically quoted.